The
Jewish Book
of Living
and Dying

The Jewish Book of Living and Dying

Lewis D. Solomon

with a foreword by
Simcha Paull Raphael

JASON ARONSON INC.
Northvale, New Jersey
Jerusalem

Grateful acknowledgment is made to the following for permission to reprint
published material:

Roberta Carson, "Mark My Words." Copyright © by Roberta Carson.
Reprinted by permission of the author.

Barry Freundel, "Yizkor, The Unending Conversation." Copyright © by Barry
Freundel. Reprinted by permission of the author.

Yonassan Gershom, *From Ashes to Healing: Mystical Encounters with the Holocaust.*
Copyright © by Yonassan Gershom. Reprinted by permission of the Edgar
Cayce Foundation.

Raymond A. Moody, Jr., *Life After Life: The Investigation of a Phenomenon—
Survival of Bodily Death.* Copyright © by Raymond A. Moody, Jr. Reprinted by
permission of MBB, Inc.

This book was set in 11 pt. Janson by Pageworks of Old Saybrook and Lyme,
CT, and printed and bound by Book-mart Press, Inc. of North Bergen, NJ.

Library of Congress Cataloging-in-Publication Data

Solomon, Lewis D.
 The Jewish book of living and dying / by Lewis D. Solomon.
  p. cm.
 Includes bibliographical references and index.
 ISBN 0-7657-6101-7
 1. Future life—Judaism. 2. Spiritual life—Judaism. 3. Intermediate
state—Judaism. 4. Jewish mourning customs. 5. Reincarnation—Judaism.
6. Judaism—Doctrines. I. Title.
 BM635.S65   1999
 296.3'3—dc21   99-20642
                                                     CIP

Printed in the United States of America on acid-free paper. For information
and catalog write to Jason Aronson, Inc., 230 Livingston Street, Northvale, NJ
07647-1726, or visit our website: www.aronson.com

DEDICATION

In memory of my mother and our conversations about canaries and the afterlife.

Contents

Contents

Contents

ACKNOWLEDGMENTS

I owe two enormous debts of gratitude. First, to my mentor Rabbi Dr. Joseph H. Gelberman, who introduced me to the concept of Spiritual Judaism. Second, to Dr. Simcha Paull Raphael and his work of monumental scholarship, *Jewish Views of the Afterlife*, which served as the source of creative inspiration for this book. All the readers of this book should consult Dr. Raphael's book for a detailed exposition of Jewish texts and tales.

Many individuals, including Robert M. Hausman, Laurence E. Mitchell, Simcha Paull Raphael, and Robert E. Sheperd, provided helpful comments as my manuscript worked its way to completion. I also want to thank the students in my Jewish Views of the Afterlife course at the Jewish Study Center in Washington, D.C., from whom I learned so much.

John Miller and Erica M. Ostlie, respectively, Reference Librarian and Interlibrary Loan Coordinator, at the Jacob Burns Law Library of The George Washington University Law School, unfailingly helped in locating hard to find materials. Dale T. Wise, Jr., my secretary, typed the manuscript with his customary diligence.

Finally, in preparing this book and using Jewish sources to develop a universally applicable model of the afterlife, I have been much encouraged by Max I. Dimont, who wrote in *Jews, God and History*:

Throughout the centuries, the trinity of Jehovah, Torah, and Prophets, by accident or design evolved two sets of laws, one to preserve the Jews as Jews, the other to preserve mankind. In their first two thousand years, the Jews used that third of the Torah. . . . which deals with priesthood and sacrifice to maintain themselves as a Jewish entity in a world of pagan civilizations. In their second two thousand years, they used that third of Torah and Talmud which deals with ritual and dietary restrictions to maintain their ethnic unity even as they spread the universal aspects of Judaic humanism. Left now of Torah and Talmud are the universal contents only—the third that deals with morality, justice, and ethics. Does this progression suggest that Judaism is now prepared to proselytize its faith in a world ready to accept its prophetic message? Is this to be the destiny of the Jews in the third act?*

*Max I. Dimont (1994). *Jews, God and History*, rev. ed., (New York: Mentor), pp. 450–451.

FOREWORD

There is a story told about the hasidic master, Reb Simcha Bunam of Pzhysha, who was close to the last moments of his life. As he lay upon his deathbed, his grief-stricken wife burst into tears. With calm equanimity, the dying Rebbe looked at her lovingly and said, "Why are you crying? My whole life was only that I might learn how to die." With these words rolling off his lips, he died peacefully, fully accepting his finite human fate.

Whenever I think about this deathbed scene, I ask myself what it would mean to spend one's whole life learning how to die. It's not an idea we think about very often. Judaism is usually seen as a life-affirming religion. From a very young age, children are taught to observe holy days and sacred moments of Jewish time. Teenagers are inducted into Jewish religious life through bar and bat mitzvah preparations, and families are admonished to participate actively in the Jewish community. Even elders are given inspirational guidelines to keep on living and enjoying life, the consequences of this being a silent denial of fears and anxieties people have about dying. Truth be told, aside from *Yizkor* memorial services, death is certainly not a major topic of discussion in Jewish life.

Basically, as a society which prides itself on life and living, we do as much as possible to avoid the topic of death. And yet, die we must! This is a reality inherent to the nature of human life.

So how can we learn how to die, or even more, to live each moment with conscious awareness of our mortality, that we may be adequately prepared to face death whenever it appears on the horizon of our life? Who will be our teachers and guides in learning how to meet death with wisdom and integrity?

It is this task Rabbi Lewis Solomon has taken on in writing *The Jewish Book of Living and Dying*. Bringing together scholarly research and his own pastoral and teaching experience, Lewis Solomon takes the reader on a journey exploring the infinite wisdom which Judaism offers on the subject of death, dying, and the afterlife journey of the soul. Synthesizing mythic and mystical Jewish writings with contemporary psychological understanding, Rabbi Solomon gives us a simple yet profound message: Death is not the end of human existence, but only a transition to another realm of consciousness. By learning more about little-known Jewish teachings on life after death, one can be more adequately prepared to deal with the encounter with dying, death, and grief.

While many Jewish teachers, texts, and traditions speak about the survival of an eternal soul, detailed information on what specifically happens to human consciousness after death is often difficult to track down. As a rule, it is easier for someone to discover what Tibetan Buddhists, Native Americans, and Roman Catholics teach about postmortem survival, than what Judaism has to say on this topic. But in *The Jewish Book of Living and Dying* you will find a clear, concise map of the afterlife journey of the soul. It is a map based on ancient Jewish wisdom which has contemporary relevance and practical application.

Death, as Rabbi Solomon notes, is not a painful event, but rather it is "like taking hair out of milk." The soul leaves behind the physical body, and enters a supernatural realm—beyond the usual limits of time, space, and geography—in which an entirely new excursion of conscious awareness ensues. The Jewish mystical view of afterlife can be best understood as a multi-stage journey of consciousness. At first there are a variety of visionary experiences—luminescent light, angelic beings, beloved friends and family, and a panoramic view of one's life experiences. Dynamic and ever-changing, this postmortem journey subsequently takes a disembodied being through a process of separation from the physical body; cleansing of unresolved emotional residue of life in a state of purgation; into a time of intellectual contemplation of heavenly bliss; and ultimately toward spiritual union with the divine, or preparation for re-embodiment, reincarnation.

Most Jews and non-Jews alike are totally unaware that Judaism has such a sophisticated multi-dimensional model of life after death. To know this cartography of the world beyond, well in advance of death, helps one deal more effectively with death, dying, and bereavement—and of course, ultimately, with life itself!

Designed as a practical death manual, *The Jewish Book of Living and Dying* provides not only a model of the hereafter, but also practical tools for assisting the dying and the bereaved. In the face of immanent death and terminal illness individuals often feel alone and afraid. Family members experience helplessness and disempowerment in what can be an overwhelming, high-tech medical environment. In applying Jewish afterlife teachings to the reality of our times, Lewis Solomon created functional Jewish resources for helping people die consciously—meditations for the death moment itself, and for assisting the soul in its afterlife journey.

Similarly, for the bereaved, you will find in this book great solace for the hurting heart. To lose a loved one, be it a parent, spouse, sibling, child, or friend, can be a deeply lonely and heart-breaking experience. In death, relationship between two human beings feels drastically severed. However, this book assumes as a given the ancient Jewish view that even after death the thread of inter-connection between the world of the living, and the world of the dead persists. Rooted in an understanding of traditional Jewish mourning rituals, Rabbi Solomon presents specific meditations and other exercises to help those in mourning continue the process of healing and resolution of grief with deceased loved ones.

Yes, death is a reality of life, often leaving in its wake the deep pain of loss and the giving up of loving attachments. But the bond between human beings transcends physical mortality. As we learn more about Jewish spirituality, we can learn to infuse our lives with a growing awareness of that divine realm beyond this world wherein our beloved ones abide. By opening the heart and mind to the invisible realms of the afterlife, we can transform mourning into meaning, heal the hurting heart, and awaken the individual soul to the deeper mysteries of life and death.

The Jewish Book of Living and Dying is a wonderful contribution to the growing body of Jewish literature on dying and death. It is a much-needed contemporary Jewish death manual. As you travel your own journey in wrestling with the human encounter with death, savor the wisdom this book provides for living a conscious spiritual life.

Simcha Paull Raphael, Ph.D.
Philadelphia, Pa.

CHAPTER ONE

INTRODUCTION

We will all die. Death for us represents the ultimate and the most terrifying mystery. In this book I try to deal with this mystery that someday will be answered for each of us—conclusively. Drawing on the Jewish tradition, I present the belief that death is not the end of life for our immortal soul.

When we are terminally ill, we become fearful. We fear pain in both the dying process and at the moment of death, as well as the post-death unknown. We're also afraid of our insignificance.

When we experience the death of a loved one, we are plunged into grief that is nearly unimaginable and inexpressible. Yet our encounter with loss and brokenheartedness is very much a part of the human experience in the world.

In our deep sorrow, it is hard to imagine there could ever be any joy in the life. We ask: Why me? How could God let this happen? It is hard to see any meaning or purpose in life. Facing death, whether your own or a loved one's, faith in life and in God is often shattered, but in everything there is meaning.

This book seeks to help you think about the meaning of death and dying in the midst of your pain, fear, grief, and loss. It presents the concept of life after death from the perspective of the Jewish tradition, one of the world's great religions.

Although it is difficult for any words to soothe you in times of emotional hurt, I hope to provide a measure of comfort to: individuals confronting terminal illness; healthy people facing the imminent death of a loved one; and the bereaved—whether young or old, grieving the death of a family member or a close friend. This book is also aimed at individuals interested in learning about the spiritual teachings of various religions, in this case Judaism, so that they can develop a more meaningful understanding of death as part of our understanding life. Thus, all spiritual seekers, whatever their religious or spiritual background, can use the Jewish conceptualization of the afterlife to help them better cope with adversity.

I only ask you to at least be open to hearing and perhaps accepting the reassuring belief that there is life beyond death. The Jewish teachings on the afterlife may help you construct a personal belief system making easier the acceptance of death—your own or a loved one.

Think about what it might be like if, as children, we were taught that after death there exists the possibility of interconnection with those who have left this world. Imagine how we might think differently about death and life if we were taught to attune to those unseen worlds beyond the physical realm we call life.

Contemplate people freely sharing their own sense of the interconnection between the world of the living and the afterlife realms of the departed. Imagine what it would be like to live in a culture where beliefs and experiences with a life beyond death were normal.

As the twenty-first century unfolds, I believe we are about to create such a world in which afterlife is understood to be an organic part of the circle of life: life, death, afterlife, and rebirth. The circle of life, unending and everchanging: life, death, afterlife, and rebirth.

In various ways, we are united with loved ones, even after death. The notion that a conscious awareness exists that humans experience after death, seems strange to our Western, rationalistic mind set. Yet at the root of this book, the Jewish tradition has long taught that bodily death is not the end of our existence.

The basic message of this book is quite simple. Throughout the ages, Jewish sages have had much to say about survival after bodily death. The Jewish tradition teaches that death does not end a soul's existence. Life—our essence, our spirit—survives the failure of the flesh. Rather, death represents a transition from one state of consciousness to another level of consciousness—a disembodied spiritual awareness.[1] After bodily death, a person's immortal soul enters several non-material realms where it undergoes a series of transformational experiences designed to help purify it and consolidate the lessons of the life just lived. Life after death thus represents an evolutionary journey of consciousness consisting of various stages of learning accompanied by an integration of the experiences from the deceased's immediate past life. Learning about the specific dynamics of this journey will help you understand more fully the enigmatic mysteries of life, death, and the world beyond.

During this post-death period prior to rebirth in a new physical body, a decedent's soul is tempered and transformed. Ultimately, almost all souls will be reborn. Thus, the concept of reincarnation is universally applicable to nearly every human being.

In short, the Jewish teachings on the afterlife offer an enduring message of hope, not despair. We, the living, should not fear death. Rather, death represents an elevation to a different and higher life plane that does not have associated with it the sufferings of the physical body. Death offers us the possibility of an ascension to a

---

[1]Jeffrey Mishlove (1993) in *The Roots of Consciousness: The Classic Encyclopedia of Consciousness Studies Revised and Expanded* (Tulsa: Oak Council Books) provides an excellent overview of consciousness exploration. The book presents an introduction to historical and contemporary consciousness studies throughout the world.

realm free from earthly hindrances. When we diminish our fear of death, however difficult for us to do, then we are born into the joy of life and the fullness of living.

Looking at the Jewish wisdom on death and the afterlife, Judaism asserts that a window, not a wall, exists between this world and the world of the dead. Drawing from the legacy of Jewish afterlife teachings, you will begin to understand that a subtle yet perceptible window of communication exists between the world of the living and the world of the dead. The living and the departed can and often do remain interconnected. This point of view, when reinfused into contemporary Jewish understanding, provides the wisdom essential for creating a spiritually-based model for dying and bereavement, necessary for the realities of life in the twenty-first century.

THE JEWISH TRADITION'S SOURCES DEALING WITH THE AFTERLIFE

Before we begin our tour of the soul's afterlife journey, it's important to keep in mind that the Jewish tradition bases its approach to the post-death survival of the soul on four sources:

1. Biblical
2. Rabbinic
3. Medieval
4. Mystical[2]

---

[2]For background on rabbinic, medieval, and mystical Judaism, I have drawn on Robert M. Seltzer (1980), *Jewish People, Jewish Thought: The Jewish Experience in History* (New York: Macmillan), pp. 243–314, 373–450; and Edward Hoffman (1992), *The Way of Splendor: Jewish Mysticism and Modern Psychology* (Northvale, NJ: Jason Aronson), pp. 7–40.

BIBLICAL

Biblical texts include the Five Books of Moses (Genesis, Exodus, Leviticus, Numbers, and Deuteronomy) as well as the Prophets, and various writings, including the Psalms and the Proverbs. These biblical texts were mainly written from the tenth to the fifth century B.C.E

RABBINIC

Rabbinic Judaism was born out of the destruction of the Second Jewish Temple in Jerusalem some 1900 years ago. For the next 500 to 900 years of the Common Era, up until the medieval period in Europe, a vast body of literature developed reflecting the creative ferment of the rabbis. The rabbinic literature consists of two parts: first, the Talmud—mainly a legalistic discourse on all aspects of Jewish life as well as nonlegal materials including teachings on the afterlife; and second, the Midrash—interpretations of various Biblical passages using allegories, parables, analogies, and stories to illustrate the meaning of verses.

The rabbis, consistent with the biblical prophetic tradition, maintained that a new Divine world order, a transhistorical human realm of world peace, social justice, and human unity, would eventually replace the existing sociopolitical realm. The rabbis' teachings mainly focused on how to live in the human community, not on interpreting the mysteries of the cosmos.

Yet, for two thousand years, the rabbinic tradition has espoused an ethical reward-and-punishment stance. Postmortem Divine judgment would be accompanied by rewards or punishments resulting from an individual's worldly actions, words, and thoughts, particularly in regard to observing an array of Jewish laws and rituals. Right conduct would lead to the reward of a blissful existence in the afterlife, a glorious suite on a cruise ship with an ocean view, if you will. While those who had opted for material gain at the expense of others would suffer the heat of the ship's boiler room.

MEDIEVAL

Medieval ways of looking at the afterlife consist of two major sources: medieval literature (including interpretative biblical Midrash) and philosophical writings. The Medieval legendary narratives written in the tenth to the fourteenth centuries of the Common Era explore a wide range of Jewish themes, including the afterlife. These visionary fantasy texts, comparable to *The Divine Comedy*, Dante's epic poem about heaven and hell, graphically portray the details of experiences after death, including the pangs of the grave, the torment of Purgatory, and the bliss of Paradise.

Along with the medieval biblical Midrash, the period between 900 to 1300 C.E. witnessed an outpouring of medieval Jewish philosophical writings, blending rabbinic Judaism with philosophy, particularly Greek philosophic thought and its belief in spiritual immortality. These writings contain teachings on the essential nature of the immortal soul and its afterlife journey. Subsequent to the writings of the Jewish medieval philosophers, we find much more extensive attention to the fate of the soul in the postmortem realms.

MYSTICAL

Mystical Jewish teachings (the Kabbalah) are products of academies of Jewish mysticism in thirteenth to fifteenth century Spain and France and sixteenth century Palestine. These writings, particularly the *Zohar* (*The Book of Splendor*), a mystical commentary on the biblical Five Books of Moses, which appeared in the late thirteenth century of the Common Era, provide some of the most sophisticated Jewish views on the afterlife. In discussing life after death, as part of the authors' interest in the big picture of the universe, these mystical writings focus on the soul; specifically, its various dimensions, its relationship to the physical body, and its capacity for transcendent awareness of the Divine. The medieval Midrash and, later, the mystical *Zohar* constitute perhaps the best and the most comprehensive multifaceted resources for understanding the Jewish views of the afterlife.

The mystical literature also encompasses the tales produced by Hasidism, a populist Jewish movement emphasizing ecstasy and joy in prayer and worship, which emerged in the eighteenth century and continues to our own day. The Hasidic movement brought mysticism to the Jewish masses and spawned the Hasidic tale, which told, in story form, the wondrous life and deeds of various charismatic Hasidic rabbis (*rebbes* —or *tzaddikim*—highly evolved, righteous spiritual leaders) beginning with the Baal Shem Tov, the founder of the Hasidic movement, who lived in Poland from 1698 to 1760. In addition to glorifying the lives and deeds of deceased *rebbes*, the Hasidic tales provide a rich source of afterlife teachings, particularly enduring spiritual beliefs about immortality and the post-death survival of the soul.

One Hasidic folktale on the soul's afterlife journey communicates Judaism's essential teaching on the world of the souls. A story is told concerning Rabbi Elimelech of Lizhensk, who lived in Poland from 1717 to 1786.[3] Reb Elimelech immersed himself in Torah study, particularly in its mystical forms based on Kabbalistic teachings. He became one of the leading figures of Hasidism.

Reb Elimelech had a close friend, Chaim, a highly accomplished, righteous person. A great friendship existed between Reb Elimelech and Chaim.

Suddenly Chaim took sick and was very close to death. When Reb Elimelech visited him, Chaim, a widower, wept and begged him,

---

[3]Adapted from Simcha Paull Raphael (1994), *Jewish Views of the Afterlife* (Northvale, NJ: Jason Aronson), pp. 394–397.

"Raise my only child, Abe, whom I will soon leave behind." At Chaim's deathbed, Reb Elimelech promised to raise Abe and educate him in the ways of the Jewish people on condition that "Chaim come to him and tell him what it's like on the other side." After shaking on this promise, Chaim passed on.

Fulfilling his commitment, Reb Elimelech raised Abe, sending him to the best schools and giving him a lavish bar mitzvah. According to the custom of the time, the Rebbe arranged a highly advantageous marriage for Abe to a rich man's daughter.

On the wedding day, the guests waited in despair for Reb Elimelech to perform the ceremony. One hour, then two went by. Looking through the keyhole of the Rebbe's study several guests saw Reb Elimelech lost in thoughts and deep meditation.

After three hours, the Rebbe emerged and performed the ceremony.

At the reception, Reb Elimelech told the guests about his agreement with Chaim. The Rebbe recounted how he had agreed to raise Abe and in return, Chaim would tell him about how he fared in judgment. Moments before the ceremony was to begin, the Rebbe related, "Chaim came to me. He seemed to me like a fully living person. I asked him, well, what was it like?"

"The moment of death," Chaim indicated, "was painless. It was like taking a hair out of milk."

After recounting how he witnessed his body being prepared for burial, Chaim focused on his unawareness of his death at the gravesite. "After they put me in my grave and covered it with earth, I wanted to leave the cemetery and go to my old house. As I started off for home, I followed a road which led across a small brook. I tried to pass through the brook, but the waters suddenly became very deep. I became afraid to go further. As the sun set, I continued to experience a fierce desire to return to my former home. Should I go or stay—there or here—what to do?"

"Then I saw a being of light and I entered the world of truth. After a life review, where I revisited every thought, word, and deed in my life, I stood for judgment before the Heavenly Tribunal. They began to weigh my record."

"I looked at the wicked in Purgatory. I saw old friends and heard their painful sobs."

"I also saw the lofty spiritual heights and the bliss of the righteous in Paradise.".

"I then spoke to a representative of the Heavenly Tribunal," Chaim related. "So, I said to him, speak to the Heavenly Tribunal and say to them that I was a good friend of Reb Elimelech, who, I believe, is so very well received by God. The representative went to the Heavenly Tribunal. They indicated that I merited a place in Paradise. However, because I had given my handshake promise to Reb Elimelech that I would come to him and tell him what happened, unless I keep my word, I won't be admitted to Paradise."

"Today, I began to go to Reb Elimelech and to keep my promise."

And Reb Elimelech finished his tale, "Chaim spoke to me and told me to tell you his story today at Abe's wedding. I asked him to stay for the ceremony and the reception, but Chaim said, 'Don't hold me back now that I've fulfilled my promise. I can't describe to you the incomparable bliss of Paradise. All earthly things are unimportant to me.'"

UNIVERSALLY APPLICABLE MODEL OF THE AFTERLIFE

This book presents a spiritually-based, universally applicable model of life after death, based on Jewish sources, accessible to and having relevance for all spiritual seekers, Jews and non-Jews. It delineates the Jewish philosophy of the soul's afterlife journey and offers spiritual guidelines for understanding the human encounter with death.

In exploring the soul's afterlife journey, this book examines: 1) guideposts for living and dying provided by Spiritual Judaism (Chapter 2); 2) what survives death, focusing on the immortal soul (Chapter 3); 3) the separation of the soul from the physical body: the process of dying and the death moment (Chapter 4); 4) the separation of the soul from the physical body: death-moment visions (Chapter 5); 5) the separation of the soul from the physical body: the pangs of the grave (Chapter 6); 6) the purification of the soul in Purgatory for a finite time period (Chapter 7); 7) the heavenly visions of the soul in Paradise (Chapter 8); 8) spiritual unification, consisting of return of the soul to the Source of Life and rebirth (Chapter 9); 9) understanding death as a means for understanding life (Chapter 10).

Our thoughts about death and the afterlife influence how we conduct (and should lead) our lives—whatever our age. Death puts our life into perspective. I want to provide you with the tools to interpret your status in life and then to alter that status, if necessary, to bring about your spiritual purification and eventually a more fortuitous afterlife passage.

At the outset, four points are noteworthy. First, this book draws mainly upon the mystical tradition, for instance, as portrayed in Reb Elimelech's folktale, reframed in terms of the universally applicable concepts of Spiritual Judaism.

As developed in Chapter 2, I write this book within the context of Judaism—what I call Spiritual Judaism, an ethical, virtue-oriented, monotheistic system[4]—beyond the minutiae of the traditional legalistic rules and rituals designed to govern everyday living.

Striving to fill our spiritual hunger, offer meaning to our exist-

---

[4]Ethical, virtue-oriented monotheism as the key concept underpinning Judaism is set forth in Leo Baeck (1948), *The Essence of Judaism*, trans. Irving Howe (New York: Schocken), and Rabbi Morris Lichtenstein (1934), *Judaism: A Presentation of Its Essence and a Suggestion for Its Preservation* (New York: Society of Jewish Science), pp. 21–34, 57–101.

ence, and a connection with the transcendent, Spiritual Judaism represents a nondogmatic, nonlegalistic path. It is a way of thought, feeling, and belief—not centered on rules, rote rituals, and prayers—about God and the spiritual depths of our being. It welcomes all peoples who seek to attune to the presence of God in their lives. It offers the vision of a personal, intimate experience of God as the source of health, joy, love, abundance, and wholeness. It is designed to help us meet the crises we all face in living and dying.

Spiritual Judaism focuses on practical spirituality—spiritual living that's liberating, that promotes and unfolds our inner human possibilities, and helps each of us realize his or her highest self and that of others around us.

Spiritual Judaism strives to answer two fundamental questions: How can I personally access, experience, and relate to God? How can I daily enhance the quality of my life and the lives of those around me through ethical conduct and the practice of certain virtues and personal attributes? Thus, Spiritual Judaism can inform our lives, thoughts, words, and deeds—whether we're 21, 30, 50, or 80. It's a profound, inspiring, life enhancing tradition.

Second, portions of six chapters of this book, namely, Chapters 4 through 9, offer soul-guiding[5] techniques designed to assist the soul on its afterlife journey. These various soul-guiding techniques will not only help a departed soul lessen the pangs of the grave in the immediate transition after death—what Chaim, Reb Elimelech's friend, experienced at the cemetery—but also promote the interconnectedness between the survivors and a decedent's soul.

These soul-guiding techniques will assist many individuals seeking to establish a new (or continue to strengthen their) relationship

---

Dr. Simcha Paull Raphael's original concept of soul guiding as a link between the world of the living and the world of the dead originated in his doctoral dissertation, Simcha Steven Paull (1986), *Judaism's Contribution to the Psychology of Death and Dying* (Ph.D. diss., California Institute of Integral Studies), pp. 349–350, 355–359, 362–364, 368–371. The theme of soul guiding is developed in Raphael, *Afterlife*, pp. 383, 387–388, 391–392.

with a departed's immortal soul, based upon a belief that a window of communication, albeit separated by some sort of thin veil, exists between the living and the dead.[6] An active bond endures between the living and the departed soul, not a wall of silence, despite the seeming finality of bodily death.

The thoughts, words, and actions of the living can impact the departed soul. Using these soul-guiding techniques, the survivors, of whatever religious or spiritual persuasion, can assist a soul in its afterlife voyage. In addition, the deceased's soul, as explained in this book, may also help the living.

Third, this book emphasizes the universally applicable aspects of Judaism, its model of the soul's afterlife journey, and various soul-guiding techniques for several reasons. Our society is more deritualized than ever before. Although Americans generally are moving away from death- and mourning-related rituals, we seek new ways to express our feelings and spirituality. Thus, this book is not written from the perspective of renewing and reinvigorating traditional Jewish death and mourning rituals (although some readers may find helpful this book's succinct distillation of these practices). Rather I want to show how spiritual seekers can use the philosophy and the concepts underlying these rituals to cope more adequately with adversity. For twenty-first century spiritual seekers, the prayers and rituals of any one religious tradition are far less important than the belief system's underlying spiritual principles.

This book seeks to meet the need for spiritual resources for dealing with death and mourning. The advances in medicine and biomedical technology have led to a vast extension of life expectancy. As our population ages, cancer, Alzheimer's, and other debili-

---

[6]Insights into apparitional encounters and communications between the living and the dead are presented in Raymond Moody, M.D. with Paul Perry (1993), *Reunions: Visionary Encounters with Departed Loved Ones* (New York: Villard). Moody presents a cogent argument, based on his observations and experiments, for our ability to contact the deceased.

tating diseases will impact more people. We also face the tragedy of lives cut short as well as individuals who experience unbearable pain and suffering as part of the dying process.

Also, as part of a growing societal quest for spiritual meaning, a widespread yearning exists for information about the afterlife and the interrelationship between the living and the departed. As one of the world's great religions, Judaism has much to say about the soul's afterlife journey for all spiritual seekers striving to understand and wrestle with the human encounter with death.

Fourth, according to the Jewish tradition, our existence has a transcendent value. The belief in spiritual survival, as the essence of our being, presents an energizing and uplifting force for the living.

Believers in the soul's afterlife survival, from my experience, are life-affirming and generally set for themselves very high standards of personal conduct and aspiration that enable them to meet life's challenges and temptations with more patience, courage, and strength. They are less prone to despair and depression.[7]

Accepting our own mortality and understanding that death is part of the human condition, represents a major step in developing a positive approach to life and living fully now. Choosing to live a "good" life, recognizing that our thoughts, words, and deeds have consequences now and for our souls in the afterlife, prepares us to accept death as part of life. Hopefully, this book will help you appreciate the meaning of life and to accept death, whether anticipated or sudden, whether painful or free of agony.

---

[7]The benefits of a belief in spiritual survival are discussed by Gary Doore (1990), "Epilogue: What Should We Believe?" in *What Survives? Contemporary Explorations of Life After Death*, ed. Gary Doore, Ph.D.(Los Angeles: Jeremy P. Tarcher), pp. 275–277.

CHAPTER TWO

GUIDEPOSTS FOR LIVING AND DYING THROUGH SPIRITUAL JUDAISM

As we stand on the edge of the twenty-first century, for many Jews, Judaism has lost its vital content.

Whenever we think about Judaism, we usually focus on observances and rules. We think that Judaism is synonymous with an almost mindless performance of ceremonies and rituals. Yet the ceremonies, rituals, and all the accompanying rules are the byways of Judaism, not its highways or its essence. For me, the rituals and rules, although designed to open and touch the spiritual dimension of life, often block my spiritual vitality. I find little value in rituals and rules for their own sake. They're spiritual choking.

In this chapter, I want to develop the concept of Spiritual Judaism, which focuses on: the One Divine Presence, adherence to ethical standards in our conduct with others, and the pursuit of personal virtues. As the prophet Micah expressed it more than 2,500 years ago: " . . . [D]o justice, and . . . love goodness, and . . . walk humbly with your God" (Micah 6:8). As you strive to formulate an approach to a "successful" Jewish-oriented life and death, where can you turn for guidance?

LOOKING ANEW AT THE TORAH

I reject the notion of a "Torah true" existence as our guidepost for: daily living; for death and dying; and for facilitating the soul's afterlife journey. Jewish fundamentalists never want to discuss or face the virtually unanimous conclusion of scholars that the Torah (the Five Books of Moses) was not given by God to Moses on Mount Sinai. Rather, the Torah achieved its familiar shape and dimensions from various human hands as the result of an evolutionary process. The books of the Old Testament were written at different times by various writers.

For the past four hundred years, critical biblical analysis has found: numerous duplications and repetitions in the Pentateuch; variations in the name of the Divine; and a broad diversity of language and style, and contrasting viewpoints in the text.

The discovery of duplication extending across a considerable body of the text, starting with two stories of creation in the Book of Genesis, led to the claim, going back in the seventeenth century, that the Torah had its own history of composition. Specifically, that it had been compiled from a number of documents.

Variations in God's Hebrew names, Elohim and Yahweh, used in the Five Books of Moses, provide further evidence of different sources.

Three parallel sources, known as E, J, and P, and the addition of a fourth source, D, gave rise to what has become known as the four-source documentary hypothesis.[1] Although scholars vigorously dispute the dates and the exact nature of the four sources, the view that four sources underpin the Torah as we know it today holds the field.

[1]The scholarly insights on documentary hypothesis are brilliantly summarized in Richard Elliot Friedman (1987), *Who Wrote the Bible?* (Englewood Cliffs, NJ: Prentice Hall).

Thus, modern, critical biblical scholarship has undermined the traditional understanding of the Torah as divinely revealed by God to Moses. Biblical scholarship called and continues to call into question two bedrock doctrines: first, a literal revelation; and second, the covenant between God and the Jews, on which much of traditional Jewish rituals and laws are based.

The authors of the Bible wove together various source material—a collection of traditions, semihistorical yarns, and sheer fantasies—originating at different times in ancient Israel. The Bible, as a human work, was authored by many humans and was subject to editing and re-editing over long periods of time.

Although the Torah has special significance for the Jewish people, these writings are not uniquely true or a superior form of Divine revelation. Rather, I suggest that we should see the Torah as a record of the spiritual life of the Jewish people and as evidence of their religious quest.

Viewing the Bible as a human product, an unverifiable mix of myth and historical fantasy, not the commanding voice of God, we need not accept either the authority of the Torah or the two thousand years of rabbinic tradition interpreting the Torah. Jewish law, as formulated by men in a patriarchical culture, should no longer provide the basic consensus for the essence of Judaism.

What this means for our daily living and ultimately, our death and dying, is quite simple. Today, we can de-emphasize the study of the Torah. We need not live in accordance with all of the supposed 613 Divine commands designed to take Jews through every aspect of living and dying as embodied in *The Code of Jewish Law (Shulchon Oruch)*—a compendium of harsh, rigid, and often archaic legalisms, centering, notably, on the observance of dietary (Kosher) laws and the Sabbath.

Viewing the Old Testament as a source from which humanity may gain deeper insights and be led to nobler conduct, the spirit of the Torah does, however, still provide guidance and inspiration for us today. But while the Hebrew Bible retains its spiritual vitality, particularly in the teachings of the prophets and the guidance provided by the Psalms and the Book of Proverbs, each of us is free to make his or her own decisions as to what laws and rituals he or she wishes (or doesn't wish) to observe and with what degree of rigor. Thus, the laws and rituals can and should be adapted to modern life.

Departing from Judaism's primary focus on traditional rules and rituals, I offer Spiritual Judaism, an ethical, virtue-oriented monotheism, as the foundation of our spiritual experience. We need to: first, think in terms of God and our relationship with God and God's relationship to each of us; second, to conduct ourselves ethically in our dealings with others; and third, to practice certain personal virtues. Let's begin by taking up the monotheistic aspect of Spiritual Judaism.

PUTTING GOD INTO OUR DAILY LIVES

In striving to revitalize Judaism, we cannot bypass the question of God. I see no alternative but to restore God to our consciousness. We need to believe in the living reality of God, but without the traditional rigidity and legalisms.[2]

God should be seen as the one God for all of humanity, a universal concept of God, accessible to all, the Source of ethical imperatives for all of humanity. Despite our ethnic, cultural, and racial diversity, we are all children of one Eternal Being, the endless One, Who is without beginning or ending, and Who is beyond time and space. Recognizing our unity and our interconnectedness, we should strive to overcome our separation and alienation from one another.

---

[2]I have drawn on Rabbi Morris Lichtenstein (1943), *Judaism: A Presentation of Its Essence and a Suggestion for Its Preservation* (New York: Society of Jewish Science), pp. 28–34.

We should also recognize that God transcends human knowledge. The Eternal far surpasses our material world and our physical selves.

God is not merely an historic figure but a present and ongoing reality. The Holy One is both transcendent, infinite and eternal, and imminent, the Divine Essence dwelling in every human heart and participating in everyone's life. God is not separate or remote from us.

God is the Source, the Creator of all reality, and the Sustainer of all reality. As the Sustainer of all, God's love and care makes all existence possible.

We seek an attunement to the Spirit, the Presence of God as the source of health, joy, love, and abundance. We know the Supreme Sovereign through our experiences. If we suffer or if we are in need or in distress, when we focus on God, through prayer, meditation, or visualization, our burdens often become lighter and our minds grow happier. In my experience and through my observation of others, informal prayer, meditation, and visualization enhance the real purpose of the worship experience, namely, achieving a closeness to God, bringing about a deeper realization of the spiritual depths of our being, producing relief to a heavy heart, animating a depressed spirit, and yielding courage and optimism.

We should realize that we live in the presence of a benevolent, merciful God. We need to realize God's presence and have faith in Divine goodness. God, the Sustainer, is near to us. The Eternal has a benevolent interest in each of us. In the midst of the strains and stresses of modern life and the perplexing and often overwhelming dilemmas and problems we all face, God remains the Sustainer to whom we can turn for guidance and for help. We can turn over our problems and our needs to God. By becoming open and receptive, we make room for God and the Eternal's gift to us.

Some find it difficult to accept the notion of any God, or a living God, in the face of evil and suffering—so much of which the

Jewish people have witnessed in the twentieth century. As we think about the mystery of evil and suffering in human lives, we are sustained by our faith and trust in a living God's presence and goodness. After the almost imaginable nightmare of the Holocaust, the Jewish people have witnessed a renaissance of religion and culture and a return to the land of Israel.

In difficult times, faith lends stability and fortitude to the human mind. Do not withdraw or be paralyzed in the face of the magnitude of evil and suffering. Although placing our lives in God's hands, pursue a pro-active, not a passive, path. Strive to diminish or eliminate evil and suffering in the world. Recognize that we all share in human suffering and that God preserves us in our plight.

Thus, even in the midst of seemingly tragic and profoundly difficult circumstances, strive to let go of our fears. No matter how difficult, try to flow gently with life's circumstances, trusting in God's wise and beneficial ways.

As we think of life as a spiritual process, beyond a deep God-consciousness and a perception of the universe as a Divine abode, conduct ourselves ethically and practice certain personal virtues. We need to ask: what deeds, words, and thoughts are appropriate in our interactions with others? We need to act with love and compassion and to speak kind words. We need to forgive others and to deal with unresolved emotional issues and botched relationships, now. We also need to be humble. In short, we need to do, say, and think the good and the beautiful. But how?

ETHICAL CONDUCT

It is important for Judaism to emphasize our ethical responsibilities. In our interactions with others, we need to conduct ourselves ethically, even in the most complex and difficult moments of our lives.

The ethics of Judaism, which have become part of our Western heritage, are as necessary and as relevant in the twenty-first century as when first delivered. Judaism molds our daily conduct, influences our relations with others, makes us more honest with the world and zealous for justice and righteousness.

A Hasidic story points to the importance of being truthful. Reb Elimelech, whom we met in a Hasidic folktale in Chapter 1, once said: "When I stand before the Heavenly Tribunal and they ask me: 'Have you studied all you should?' I'll answer 'No!' Then they'll inquire: 'Have you prayed all you should?' Again, I will respond: 'No!' I'll also answer 'No' to their third question: 'Have you done all the good you should?' They'll pronounce the verdict: 'You told the truth. Therefore, you merit a share in the world to come.'"[3]

In addition to being just and truthful in all of our relationships and interactions, strive to perform good deeds, namely, living in a loving, compassionate, and forgiving manner.

LOVE AND COMPASSION

Spiritual Judaism rests on bringing us into an ideal relationship with others.[4] We are here to express love, which draws people together. We are here to be the presence of love.

Be a vehicle through which our lives express more love in the world. As Elizabeth Kübler-Ross, who transformed the way we think about death and dying, puts it; " . . . [L]ove is the sole purpose of life. . . . The ultimate lesson is learning how to love and be loved."[5]

---

[3]Adapted from Martin Buber (1975), *Tales of Hasidim: The Early Masters*, trans. Olga Marx (New York: Schocken), p. 253.

[4]Lichtenstein, *Judaism*, pp. 64–71.

[5]Elizabeth Kübler-Ross, M.D. (1997), *The Wheel of Life: A Memoir of Living and Dying* (New York: Scribner), pp. 161, 285.

Each day we need to be loving and compassionate. We need to realize that any one we meet represents a holy encounter. We need to recognize that we love best when we have as much regard for others as we have for ourselves. In other words, only in giving love will we receive it in return.

Love is inherent in us. It resides in the depths of each human heart. It is intertwined with the roots of our being. Everyone has within him or her a spark of God's love. Love of humanity represents an all-embracing, transcendent expression of the Divine.

In one of the most often cited biblical verses, the authors of the Torah tell us, "Love your neighbor as yourself . . . ." (Leviticus 19:18). This admonition represents one of the oldest expressions of the "Golden Rule." At the beginning of the Common Era, when Hillel, one of the greatest of the early Jewish sages, was asked to briefly sum up the Torah, the Talmud recounts that he replied, "What is hateful to you, do not do to your fellow"(Shabbat 31a). You needn't have any kinship or even friendship with a neighbor or another fellow human. He or she may not contribute to your happiness or well-being. You may not know him or her well or at all.

Act toward your neighbor or another human being with the same feeling, with the same selflessness, with the same devotion that you would want him or her to have if the circumstances were reversed.

"Love your neighbor" means feeling a deep connection with and compassion for others. Feel toward others as you would have them feel to you. As a famous Hasidic rabbi, Shmuel Shmelke of Nikolsburg—who lived from 1726 to 1778 and traced his ancestry back to the prophet Samuel—expressed it, "What is hateful to you in your neighbor, don't yourself do."[6]

We can all learn the need of truly loving our neighbors from a conversation between two villagers that Rabbi Moshe Leib of Sassov—the most prominent disciple of Rabbi Shmelke of Nikols-

[6]Adapted from The Hasidic Anthology: Tales and Teachings of the Hasidim (1987), ed. and trans. Louis I. Newman (Northvale, NJ: Jason Aronson), p. 222.

burg, who lived from 1745 to 1807 and was popularly known as the Sassover Rebbe—related:

First villager: "Tell me, friend Ivan, do you love me?"

Second villager: "I love you deeply."

First villager: "Do you know what gives me pain?"

Second villager: "How can I know what gives you pain?"

First villager: "If you do not know what gives me pain, how can you say that you truly love me?"

"Understand my friends," the Sassover Rebbe concluded, "to love, truly to love, means to know what brings pain to your neighbor."[7]

Love also precludes prejudice and intolerance with respect to all peoples, all races, all religions, and all nationalities. As we are told in the Torah, "When a stranger resides with you in your land, you shall not wrong him or her. The stranger who resides with you shall be to you as one of your citizens; you shall love him or her as yourself. . . . " (Leviticus 19:33–34).

Love involves a deep consideration for others. Welcome the stranger, extend hospitality to one who comes from another land, who speaks with a foreign tongue, and who has different manners.

Become conscious of the unity of all human beings. We are all one. Despite our surface differences, we all have the same heart, the same feelings, and the same aspirations. As Jewish tradition teaches, we all have a spark of the Divine goodness and kindness within us.

MEETING THE LOVINGKINDNESS CHALLENGE

Despite these lofty and noble aspirations, the challenge of loving others is a difficult one. None of us can pretend to consistently

[7]*Ibid.*, p. 221.

be able to bring a loving perspective to every situation in our lives. As we all realize, it does not take a great deal of effort to love "good" people—your friends or those we like. The real test is loving those who may not be as "good" in our eyes—those we don't like or even those who hate us.

Put this way, love and fear must be contrasted. Love represents a giving and a sharing with others. Fear—the absence of love—cripples our capacity for giving and sharing by draining our energies from positive efforts to assist others into negative efforts to serve ourselves.

Love thus represents an infinite, all-encompassing energy pattern that should replace fear in our lives, particularly in dealing with difficult people. If we let go of our fear, then love remains. We can get rid of our fear of others by opening our hearts to love.

Let our love for others serve as our priority in every situation. Because our generous love for others is dynamic, not static—in that this type of love evolves, grows, and matures—our unconditional, selfless love for others should represent one of our key lifelong values.

Strive to be love-finders, not fault-finders. Don't focus on what's wrong or lacking in our lives or in others. Whenever we engage in fault-finding, whether in its subtle forms—for example, complaining or worrying—or its more overt forms—such as attacking others, or being judgmental or critical—we feel isolated, separated from other humans and from the goodness of life.

There's an iron law of fault-finding. Think of some of the fault-finders you know. The more they complain, the more they seem to have to complain about.

Being a love-finder means opening our hearts, our minds, and our eyes to see the wonder that's around us. There's something good and beautiful in everyone. There's something noble in each soul, some tenderness and softness in each heart, some wholesomeness in every mind. See in others their goodness and the beneficent reaches of their souls.

We're all God's children ready to do the Eternal's will. We're all expressions of the same Fountain of Life. The same Divinity is present in each of us. We are all one; unity is our natural state.

There's a Divine spark in each of us. Sometimes, this spark is difficult to find, but it's there.

Make an effort to penetrate into the Divine depths of the nature of others. See the beauty each human soul possesses. If you see others in the light of love as the children of God, you will come to love others. If you expect the best in people, if you see another's innocence, that's what he or she will show you. The more we love others, the more love will flow into us.

FORGIVENESS

Love and forgiveness are interrelated.[8] You experience love by accepting and extending forgiveness to others. By forgiving others, you'll open your heart and rediscover the capacity to love that is within you. Forgiveness represents your capacity to love even when your mind resists love.

The notion of forgiving and forgetting goes back at least as far as the sixth century B.C.E. prophet, the Second Isaiah, who advises: "I gave my back to the floggers and my cheeks to them who tore out my hair. I did not hide my face when they insulted and spat at me. For God will help me; therefore I feel no disgrace; therefore, I have set my face like a flint, and I know that I shall not be ashamed," (Isaiah 50:6–7).

Jewish sages have repeatedly emphasized forgiveness. For instance, the Talmud reports that Mar Zutra used to say daily at his bedtime: "If anyone has hurt or wronged me, they are forgiven" (*Megillah* 28a).

---

[8]I have drawn on various articles on forgiveness from *On Course* magazine by Rev. Dr. Diane Burke and Rev. Jon Mundy, two of my instructors at The New Seminary.

Every situation offers us the chance to reunite with the love within us that is our true nature and the true source of our joy and fulfillment. Every human has the same need and longing for love— the essence of our being. See our pure spiritual soul which is inherently good, and the holiness, the spark of the Divine in others who are calling out for love from us. We are all united with and connected to God. We all want to experience joy and happiness and avoid pain and suffering.

Whatever is not an expression of love on the part of another— selfishness, anger, or cruelty, to take several examples—represents a plea for help, a cry for love. You experience love by extending forgiveness to others, by accepting others, and letting go of the past.

Contemplate a past or present interpersonal problem, situation, interaction, or relationship. Think of choosing forgiveness in the face of being tempted to perceive thoughtless deeds and hurtful words as an attack on you by another and to respond with your own counterattack.

We've all experienced the physical or emotional discomfort, even the pain, of another's unkind deeds and words (for instance, a co-worker who takes all the credit for a shared project). The body grows tense, the mind becomes tight, and the heart closes. We're tempted to dislike someone, to become bitter, to hold a grudge, or even to desire revenge or vengeance.

In forgiving others, we cannot pretend that we're not affected by someone's acts or speech. Forgiveness is not permissiveness; it's not an expression of "anything goes." By forgiving, you don't pronounce as acceptable someone's cruelty, thoughtlessness, or inhumanity.

Others utter words or do things, whether intentionally or negligently, out of ignorance or forgetfulness, often out of fear, that are unkind and unloving. These actions or statements bring suffering not only to the actors or speakers, but also to others—to us. Forgiveness does not mean condoning or justifying such actions or statements. You can't ignore others' difficult qualities or hurtful acts or words.

Forgiveness means saying "no more" from a calm, quiet place. You needn't acquiesce in or endure injustice or another's harmful words or deeds. Forgiveness means sharing your concerns with another person—discussing what you see as his or her "faults."

Consider two situations. All of us can see that it's one thing to forgive a blind person who trips over you or steps on your foot. If a blind person stands on your foot and hurts you, you'll naturally ask him or her to step off your foot. You'd make your request calmly, without malice.

Let's take a much more difficult situation. Victims of child abuse—whether verbal, physical, or sexual—often indicate that forgiveness, in the sense of letting go of their focus on another's guilt, enables them to find inner peace. Realizing that their parents did the best they could, lets child abuse victims be at peace in their hearts.

Forgiveness by child abuse victims, as it does for many others, takes time. They need to be gentle with themselves to allow layers of grief, pain, and vengefulness develop into awareness and a healing transformation.

Ultimately, some child abuse victims arrive at an understanding about what their parents did to them and what their feelings are about it. Recognizing the need to move beyond the past validates their capacity to move beyond. Forgiveness brings closure.

Through forgiveness, you accept people who have disappointed you by not being perfect. You show that you're willing to let go of your focus on another's guilt and of the way you've been looking at a situation, an interpersonal problem or a relationship, and not hold on to the past. Don't let your anger and your hate continue to poison you.

You'd be amazed if you saw your unforgiving face in a mirror. The ugliness and hatred would shock you. You'd recognize the price you're paying for your unwillingness to let go of the past.

Strive to see things differently and look beyond another's body, behavior, speech, and personality. Try to go beneath the surface differences that seem to separate you from another to the more profound reality, to the deeper truth of the love each of us shares with our fellow human beings.

See another in the light of love. Perceive another's essence, his or her innocence, wholeness, and fundamental worth, deserving of your compassion, understanding, and lovingkindness.

Try to look at others for who they really are. See others as the children of God. Perceiving the God within all of us, you'll be better able to forge a sense of connection with others.

A summer camp story illustrates the importance of change in perception as a key to forgiveness. An eight-year-old boy received in the mail a box of homebaked cookies from his parents. After eating a few of them, he put the rest under his bed. The next day, when he went to get a cookie, the box was gone. All the camp counselors were told of the theft.

That afternoon, one of the camp counselors saw another boy eating the stolen cookies. He sought out the boy whose cookies had been stolen and told him, "I know who took your cookies, but will you help me teach him a lesson?" The boy replied, "OK, but won't you punish him?" The counselor explained, "Punishment will only make him hate you and resent me. Call home and ask your parents to send you another box of cookies."

The boy phoned home and in a few days received a second box of cookies. The counselor said, "Now, the boy who took your cookies is sitting near the baseball diamond. Go over there and share your cookies with him."

The boy protested. "But try it," the counselor stated, "and see what happens."

Later that afternoon, the counsellor saw the two boys walking arm-in-arm. The boy who took the cookies was trying to get the other to accept his pocket knife in repayment for the stolen cookies.

The other refused the gift from his new friend, indicating a few cookies weren't that significant.

Although difficult, you should realize that others' hurtful deeds and words—their anger, cruelty, jealously, lust, fear, pride, anxiety, thoughtlessness, or selfishness—may deep down be a plea for love. As another calls out, you should meet their cries as the expression of a desire to be healed, not to be blamed or attacked or judged harshly.

Each of us has the same need and longing for love, healing, and inner peace. We all want to make a difference and release our potential for love. See another human being through the eyes of love and compassion, not the mindset of judgmentalism and punishment. Try to answer another's acts and words with lovingkindness and compassion.

PERSONAL VIRTUES

We need to practice certain virtues in our daily lives. Two key personal attributes are: being humble as well as finding a meaningful, balanced life. By pursuing these virtues, we bring peace and harmony into our inner lives.

HUMILITY

One of our most important virtues is our humility. Decrying conceit and recognizing that we're not fully in charge of our lives, Judaism celebrates humility. As Rabbi Elimelech of Lizhensk put it: "The top of the ladder leading to perfection is humility. The person who has it has everything else."[9] Humility represents a special virtue of the Jewish leaders and sages throughout the ages.

---

[9]Adapted from *The Hasidic Anthology*, p. 185.

The legendary Moses, despite all of his extraordinary talents and achievements—his defense of his people in repeatedly arguing their case before God, his organizational skills, his formulation of monotheism, and his political leadership—was aware of his inadequacy for the task he was supposed to accomplish. Stated differently, perhaps Moses' most important characteristic was his humility. Moses is described as "a very humble man, more humble than anyone else on earth" (Numbers 12:3).

At the Burning Bush, Moses asked God, "I am nobody. How can I go to Pharaoh and bring the Israelites out of Egypt?" God responded, "I will be with you. . . ." (Exodus 3:11–12).

Moses was still unsatisfied and asked for proof. After God told him what to say to the people, Moses still had his doubts. "What if they do not believe me and do not listen to me? . . . ," Moses asked (Exodus 4:1). Even after God showed Moses signs and gave him a staff with which to perform magical wonders, Moses still hesitated. He offered excuses, "Please, O God, I have never been a man of words. . . . , I am slow of speech and slow of tongue" (Exodus 4:10), hoping God would choose someone else.

Moses' hesitation to take on the task of leading his people is similar to the reluctance later expressed by the great Hebrew prophets—for example, Amos (Amos 7:14), the First Isaiah (Isaiah 6:5), and Jeremiah (Jeremiah 1:6). They doubted their abilities and asked God to find others. These ancient prophets feared that they were incapable of doing what God asked of them. Their hesitation arose out of genuine humility. Their humility was proof of their real strengths and of their loyalty to God.

Judaism celebrates humility. The humble will be rewarded. God loves the humble and the lowly. In Book of Proverbs we read that the Eternal shows them grace (Proverbs 3:34). According to the prophet Isaiah, the humble will have cause to rejoice in God (Isaiah 29:19). Honor will come to those, the author of Proverbs writes, who are humble (Proverbs 29:23).

Jewish Wisdom Literature, the Psalms and the Proverbs, re-proaches the prideful and emphasizes what awaits proud individuals. The Psalmist reminds us that God despises the haughty and the proud (Psalm 101:5). The Book of Proverbs equates pride with foolishness (Proverbs 14:3). The proud will be humiliated (Proverbs 29:23). The Eternal will punish those who are prideful (Proverbs 15:25).

Detesting haughtiness and aloofness, humanity loves those who display genuine humility. We adore those who are humble.

A person who is modest and sympathetic to everyone generally receives, from my experience, praise from everyone. We respect someone who acts unassumingly, making no effort to evoke envy or admiration.

However, the past fifty years have brought a considerable measure of wealth to many Jews in the United States. We see manifestations of ostentation, pretentiousness, and display. As our possessions cause our hearts to swell, wealth becomes an evil weapon, destroying our character. We gain the respect of others through our humility, by acting unassumingly, not through our chutzpah, our brashness.

In the Jewish tradition, humility connotes the absence of pride—a diminished sense of self-importance—not meekness. Each of us needs to strive to achieve a balance between being self-effacing yet developing and maintaining our self-esteem and a positive self-image.

FINDING A MEANINGFUL, BALANCED LIFE

We also need to start by reflecting on what our lives are all about. There's much more than our everyday physical world. There's a transcendent meaning beyond our materialistic culture and our earthly bodies.

As we search for a way to meet our deeper needs, increased

knowledge and awareness from within the Jewish tradition and other belief systems provide a means to rethink our values and our goals. As we become more aware of our potential and our essence, we become cognizant of the trade-offs we make in our daily quest for material existence and progress.

Many of us search for a calling. In our work-a-day world, we want to do something meaningful and significant. We seek to find our bliss—here and now—which will enable us, fully using our capabilities, to make a genuine contribution, not only to our personal development but also to the well-being of humanity. Striving to be of genuine service to others, we want to make the world a better place than when we found it.

We want to find the meaning, the purpose of what our life's about—some work that has to be done, some outlet for our talents and energies. We need to strive and struggle for a worthwhile goal. But how?

Each of us needs to discover his or her bliss, his or her destiny, here and now. The more clearly you can follow your life's purpose, what you understand to be your unique function here on earth, the more your life will have meaning.

Our talents and gifts are very varied. Some have musical or artistic abilities. Others can express themselves in words. Some have a talent for making people laugh. Some love to cook and entertain. Others have a knack for gardening. Some work well with their hands; they enjoy building or repairing things. Some have a special way with kids. Others are great with animals.

Each of us has a unique and special place in God's creation. A place only each of us can fill.

Your purpose need not be on some grand scale, such as becoming a national political leader, a world-famous entertainer, or athlete. Rather, your destiny may be to be a good parent or spouse, an effective teacher, or a contributor to community betterment, or to use a skill in some form of artistic endeavor or creative expression.

How can each of us discover our destiny, our bliss, here and now? Beyond the rather mechanical inventories of skills, likes and dislikes, ask and try to answer some basic questions: What really matters, what is truly important and meaningful in our life? What do we value most deeply? How do we really want to live our lives? What activities and relationships enhance and nourish us and which do not?

Pay attention to the "call" of our destiny. In an era when nearly everyone wants to speak and few of us really want to listen, be quiet long enough to hear and abide God's clear call to us. The Divine will reveal to each of us our special purpose. Finding your destiny will not only assist you in charting your life but also, hopefully, enable you to serve others.

We also need a less materialistic orientation to life. As a practical matter, this is not easy in modern Western society. We are not going to turn, en masse, into ascetics in the twenty-first century. Society is not going to turn back the clock to the medieval world, to the era before the Industrial Revolution. We are not going to give up our material base (food, clothing, shelter, medical advancements, and education), our creature comforts, or our technological advances.

Asceticism is not the Jewish way. There's no need to suppress human needs and desires or to renounce the world. Human joy is not incompatible with holiness.

Yet, we need to turn away, at least to some degree, from our contemporary, rather one dimensional, consumer-oriented approach to life. Our desire for nonessential luxuries breeds discomfort in the human heart, taxing our strength and our resources, bringing no return in happiness.

Many of us want to reach out and attain "greater," non-material ideals. Increasingly, we see that simplicity as a lifestyle, coupled with moderation in eating, drinking, and in the pursuit of pleasure, brings contentment, lessens our worries, and brings peace of mind. Simplicity means eliminating nonessentials. We need to realize that our material needs are few, our genuine wants are quite limited.

We also need to perceive the impermanence of everything in this world. Everything changes; everything is in flux. Everything that comes into being—each of us—will pass away.

This new consciousness hopefully will lead us to a better balance in life combining a sound material base with a striving to achieve personal emotional and intellectual development as well as spiritual fulfillment. The search for a more balanced approach, integrating both the material and the spiritual aspects of life, involves an ongoing personal reexamination of the "right" use of your time, your energies, your money, and your possessions. If you want you can find the time for the people, the activities, and the values you really cherish.

Striving to live a life of greater balance and moderation, hopefully will lead us to ask what material base each of us really requires to meet our needs while enabling each of us to give more fully of ourselves to others. You need to ask: How much money and how many material possessions do you need to help you fulfill your path, your destiny, your bliss in your earthly life? In answering this question, you may lessen your urge for materialistic consumption and your desire to try to impress others by spending and consuming. You may be led to bring your expenditures in line with your values and your life purpose.

A less materialistic lifestyle provides benefits for you now and in the afterlife. As developed in Chapter 6, the Jewish mystics realized that less attachment to the material world—characterized by liberation from the demons of greed, desire, and envy—makes it easier to die peacefully, thereby lessening the pangs of the grave (what Reb Elimelech's friend Chaim experienced at the cemetery in Chapter 1). An ethical God-centered life was (and continues to be) regarded as a highly useful strategy to prepare for a painless, peaceful demise.

A more spiritually-oriented lifestyle will, Jewish sages indicate, also facilitate the soul's journey through Purgatory and Paradise. As Rabbi Pinchas Shapiro of Koretz—a Hasidic master who lived in

Russia from 1728 to 1790 and was one of the closest disciples of the Baal Shem Tov—put it: "All the pleasures come to you from your share in Paradise. The more you enjoy in this world, the less will remain for you in the World to Come. Be wise and restrain yourself in the pursuit of pleasures. Leave a portion of your enjoyment for the everlasting afterlife."[10]

None of us needs a spiritual master or guru to light our way. Rather, for our lives now and for the benefit of our souls in the hereafter, following the guideposts of Spiritual Judaism, we need to: be loving and compassionate; practice forgiveness; be humble and modest; and find a meaningful, balanced lifestyle.

Striving to put an ethical, virtue-oriented monotheism back as the centerpiece of our spiritual experience, we must realize, however difficult it is for us to admit, that no one religion possesses the unique, ultimate truth about God. I do not regard Judaism as the fullest and best expression of God's will or Jews as the Eternal's chosen people. Although affirming the distinctiveness of Judaism's heritage and role of Jews in facilitating the healing of the world and the completion of creation, acknowledge the validity of other religions. Thus, I humbly offer my vision of Spiritual Judaism as one faith among many.

---

[10]*Ibid.*, p. 2.

CHAPTER THREE

WHAT SURVIVES DEATH:
THE IMMORTAL SOUL

Nearly all of us have difficulty imagining our own death and grappling with the question of life after death. But let's try. If someone were to ask you, what happens after death? Is there life after death? How would you respond?

A rather materialistic view of human existence now predominates with respect to questions relating to death and the afterlife. Some might respond with the very matter of fact viewpoint: "Dead is dead." A human's existence ends, the brain turns to vanilla pudding after death, and the worms eat you. As a corollary, you might assume that after death any and all channels of communication and interconnection between the living and the deceased are forever ended.

Expressing this nihilistic view of death as annihilation, Rabbi Richard L. Rubenstein writes:

> I am convinced that I [had] arisen out of nothingness and am destined to return to nothingness. All human beings were locked in the same fatality. In the final analysis, omnipotent nothingness was lord of all

creation. Nothing in the bleak, cold, unfeeling universe is remotely concerned with human aspiration and longing. . . . Only death perfects life and ends its problems. God can only redeem us by slaying. We have nothing to hope for beyond what we are capable of creating in the time allotted to us. . . . [I]n the final analysis all things crumble away into the nothingness which is at the beginning and which is at the end of creation.[1]

Others would avoid any discussion of the afterlife because Judaism celebrates life, here and now. Rabbi Abraham Joshua Heschel, the charismatic twentieth century Jewish scholar, writer and religious leader, who played a highly visible role in the front ranks of the civil rights and anti-war movements of the 1960s, responded to the question of life after death as follows:

I think that's God's business what to do with me after life. Here it's my business what to do with my life. So I leave it to Him. I am so busy trying to live a good life and don't always succeed, that I have no time to worry about what God's going to do with me once I'm in the grave.[2]

If pushed, you might indicate that a deceased person's thread of life is perpetuated through his or her descendants or his or her good deeds. Children and grandchildren often reflect a decedent's personality—his or her emotional or intellectual qualities—or they bear a striking physical resemblance to the deceased. In his classic work, *Peace of Mind*, Rabbi Joshua Loth Liebman writes:

Our living immortality is found more concretely in our children, in our children's children. We may not be sculptors, able to hew immor-

[1]Richard L. Rubenstein (1996), "The Making of a Rabbi" in *Varieties of Jewish Belief*, ed. Ira Eisenstein (New York: Reconstructionist Press), pp. 179, 194–195.
[2]*The Eternal Light: A Conversation with Dr. Abraham Joshua Heschel*, NBC/TV Network, National Broadcasting Co., Inc., February 4, 1973.

tal statues out of immobile rock. Most of us, however, have the infinitely greater privilege . . . of molding the spiritual life and destiny of the generations that come after us. Men and women whom we influence by the example of our lives, the children who are touched by the flame of our spirits—it is in them that we live on and find our eternal significance.[3]

A departed is also remembered, and thus may live on, through the acts of goodness and lovingkindness he or she performed or in the profound way he or she touched the lives of those who remain on earth.

IMPACT OF MAIMONIDES

In the Jewish tradition, the contemporary, materialistic approach may stem from the influence of Maimonides, a vitally important twelfth century C.E. Jewish philosopher-scholar and codifier of Jewish law who lived from 1135 to 1204. In his philosophical works, Maimonides sought to systematically set forth the principles of Judaism in light of rationalistic Greek philosophy. In striving to demonstrate that religion and philosophy point to the same truth, Maimonides' writings continue to serve as a primary basis for Jewish learning and to impact modern Jewish thinking in numerous areas, including views of death and the afterlife.

Maimonides affirms the existence of an immortal, but disembodied, soul in the post-death World to Come, which he views as a different plane of consciousness.[4] Maimonides portrays the World

---

[3]Joshua Loth Liebman (1946), *Peace of Mind* (New York: Simon and Schuster), p. 141.

[4]Simcha Paull Raphael (1994), *Jewish Views of the Afterlife* (Northvale, NJ: Jason Aronson), pp. 249–254.

to Come as a blissful, harmonious, and transcendent realm where direct communication occurs between a deceased's soul and the Divine. However, Maimonides describes this otherworldly realm as completely beyond human comprehension. Maimonides states:

> As to the blissful state of the soul in the world to come, there is no way on earth in which we can comprehend or know it. For in this earthly existence we only have knowledge of physical pleasure; and it is for this that we long. But the bliss of the life hereafter is exceedingly great, and can only metaphorically be compared with earthly enjoyments. In reality, however, there is no comparison between the bliss of the soul in the life hereafter and the gratification afforded to the body on earth by food and drink. That spiritual bliss is unsearchable and beyond compare.[5]

Based on his view of the gap between and the duality of the body and the spirit, which occupy two separate realms, Maimonides successfully convinced many Jews to accept the view that humans lack the ability to contemplate life after death. Except for those trained in sophisticated philosophical thought, Maimonides asserted (and many Jews bought into the notion) that humans cannot understand the post-death World to Come. The view that this post-death spiritual realm is beyond human comprehension has persisted among many Jewish commentators for nearly nine hundred years.

However, over the course of millennia, Judaism, particularly Jewish mysticism, has been concerned with what happens after death. Judaism traditionally has accepted the notion of some sort of life after death. Before embarking on a tour of the afterlife spiritual world, we must ask: What is it in each human that survives death and ultimately is reborn? The Jewish tradition supplies two basic

[5]Moses Maimonides (1937), *The Mishneh Torah*, vol. 1, *The Book of Knowledge*, ed. and trans. Moses Hyamson (New York: Bloch), p. 91a.

answers: first, our body through physical resurrection; and, second, our spirit, our essence, in other words, our immortal soul.

ONE POSSIBILITY: PHYSICAL RESURRECTION

The Jewish tradition initially focused on survival through resurrection. Resurrection connotes a rebirth of the dead through Divine intervention. Through resurrection, both a decedent's body and soul would be brought back to life and thereupon judged for his or her previous deeds.[6]

The concept of resurrection originated in the late Biblical period.[7] To make a long and rather convoluted story short, although insistent on the concept of resurrection, the Biblical writers could not resolve the dichotomy between an individual or a collective resurrection. The late eighth century B.C.E. prophet Isaiah offers the hope of resurrection and reward for righteous individuals (Isaiah 26:19). The author of *Book of Daniel*, composed in about the second century B.C.E., reflecting a belief in personal resurrection, states: "Many of those that sleep in the dust of the earth will awake, some to eternal life, others to reproaches, to everlasting abhorrence" (Daniel 12:2).

Other writers of the Biblical period took a different approach to the concept of resurrection. The prophet Ezekiel, exiled by the Babylonians in about 550 B.C.E., saw a valley filled with very dry

---

[6]Neil Gillman (1997), in *The Death of Death: Resurrection and Immortality in Jewish Thought* (Woodstock, Vt.: Jewish Lights Publishing), after tracing the evolution of the idea of immortality through Jewish history and thought, argues in favor of the concept of resurrection, noting that as his body is indispensable to his sense of his own being, then God's plans for him in the afterlife must include his body. The notion of the resurrection of the dead is supported in Maurice Lamm (1969), *The Jewish Way in Death and Mourning* (New York: Jonathan David), pp. 228–233.

[7]Raphael, *Afterlife*, pp. 68–74.

human bones, presumably a battlefield containing the remains of slaughtered Jews. In a vision, Ezekiel perceived the miraculous transformation of the dry bones into living human beings:

> And God said to me: "O mortal, these bones are the whole House of Israel. They say, 'Our bones are dried up, our hope is gone; we are doomed.' Prophesy, therefore, and say to them: Thus said God: 'I am going to open your graves and lift you out of the graves, O My people, and bring you to the land of Israel" (Ezekiel 37:11–12).

For Ezekiel, in this celebrated vision of the "Valley of Dry Bones," resurrection applies to a group, the nation of Israel. In the Biblical period, it is fair to conclude that the collective fate of the Jewish people, as exemplified by Ezekiel, was more important than any individual's post-death destiny.

Resurrection of the dead emerged as central to the rabbinic worldview forming a baseline for their theological thinking.[8] In the mainstream of rabbinic literature, the notion of a collective resurrection predominates. For these writers, a collective resurrection would take place at "the end of days," marked by the arrival of the Messiah. Ushering in a new Divine world order and an earthly utopian era, the Messiah would bring about a collective resurrection. Graves would be opened, bodies would arise with souls restored, completing the resurrection of the dead of the nation of Israel.

Incorporated into the daily prayers for Jewish worship services, the doctrine of the physical resurrection of the dead has served as a key tenet—dogma, if you will—of traditional Judaism for two millennia. However, the rabbis lacked agreement on who will be resurrected at the "end of days": everyone, all righteous individuals, or only righteous Jews. However, faith in the notion of a physical resurrection provided comfort and hope for many Jews throughout the ages.

---

[8]Ibid., pp. 156–160.

In the twentieth century, most Jews have abandoned a literal belief in a physical resurrection. Death represents a breakdown of the body's physical and chemical structure. Notion of resurrection has become even more implausible in the post-Holocaust world. After the cremation of millions of physical bodies by the Nazis and the scattering of those ashes, it is difficult to fathom how these nonexistent bones can ever rise again.

OUR IMMORTAL SOUL

Modern scientific evidence seems to point to the existence of an immortal soul.[9] After reviewing the growing body of literature dealing with the scientific investigation of the near death experience over the past twenty five years, one commentator concludes: "It is difficult to analyze this evidence in depth and to come away with any other impression but that science has indeed stumbled on data of the soul."[10]

Similarly, long ago the Jewish mystics, although downplaying the doctrine of bodily resurrection, focused on the survival of a departed person's soul, an individual's invisible essence, linking each of us to God. Recognizing that we are more than our physical body, the Jewish mystics developed their concept of the soul based on the works of the medieval philosophers.

Maimonides, for example, sets forth a three-part division of the soul into: first, the vegetative aspect which governs our eating and sexual activity; second, the sensory aspect which controls our movements, our various perceptions, including hearing, seeing, smelling,

---

[9]Evidence of a nonlocal mind, beyond time and space, is presented in Larry Dossey, M.D. (1989), *Recovering the Soul: A Scientific and Spiritual Search* (New York: Bantam), pp. 123–208.

[10]Patrick Glynn (1997), *God: The Evidence: The Reconciliation of Faith and Reason in a Postsecular World* (Rocklin, CA: Prima), p. 136.

and tasting, and our imagination; and third, the rational or intellectual aspect, the power of reasoning. Maimonides viewed the vegetative and sensory aspects as disintegrating on the death of our physical body. For Maimonides, our immortal rational faculty experiences the World to Come, as described earlier in this chapter.[11]

Building on medieval philosophical thought, the Jewish mystical model portrays the soul as one unified whole, one totality consisting of interrelated fields of awareness and conscious energy connecting each individual to God. Although difficult to describe in words on printed page, Jewish mystics view the soul—our inner substance, our spirit, our higher level of consciousness—as consisting of four intertwined energy fields or levels: physical; emotional; intellectual; and spiritual.[12]

First, the physical level, a field of vital energy in each human being, which attaches to the physical body, animating and preserving it. This aspect of our soul directs the functions of our organs and orders our vital processes. For instance, our heart beats without any effort on our part and, in return, each heart beat supplies blood, the source of vitality, throughout the human body. The physical level serves as the biological life force linking each human to the earthly world.

---

[11]Raphael, *Afterlife*, p. 250.

[12]In formulating my concept of the soul, I have drawn from David Aaron (1997), *Endless Light: The Ancient Path of the Kabbalah to Love, Spiritual Growth, and Personal Power* (New York: Simon and Schuster), pp. 84–97; Rabbi Morris Lichtenstein (1970), *Peace of Mind* (New York: Society of Jewish Science), pp. 304–312; Raphael, *Afterlife*, pp. 278–280, 365–368; Rabbi David A. Cooper (1997), *God Is a Verb: Kabbalah and The Practice of Mystical Judaism* (New York: Riverhead), pp. 95–99, 106–107; Rabbi Yonassan Gershom (1992), *Beyond the Ashes: Cases of Reincarnation from the Holocaust* (Virginia Beach, VA: A.R.E. Press), pp. 179–190; Gershon Winkler (1982), *The Soul of the Matter: A Psychological and Philosophical Study of the Jewish Perspective on the Odyssey of the Human Soul Before, During and After "Life"* (New York: The Judaica Press), pp. 7-8.

The physical level, which animates our actions, gives each of us a sense that our actions are meaningful, that they can make a difference. In addition to providing meaning to our actions, the physical level makes us aware of good and bad. Almost all of us are motivated to do good, not evil, but we sometimes miss the mark.

Second, the emotional level, a field of emotional energy, which fills the heart with love, sympathy, tenderness, and compassion, represents the locus of a human's personality. This emotional level, sometimes characterized as emotional awareness, links the soul's physical level with its higher intellectual and spiritual aspects.

The soul's emotional level gives us a sense of truth and that our words can convey this truth. Just as our actions have meaning, so our words have meaning. If we wish, our words can capture this truth, a set of universal guiding principles.

Third, the mental (or intellectual) level, a mental energy field as well as the energy of the transpersonal (nonphysical) self, connects each of us to the higher spiritual aspects of our existence. The mental level is the invisible source of the mind's thoughts and inspirations. Each of us is a channel through which our intellectual powers flow.

This mental level of awareness serves as a bridge between the human and the Divine realms. The development of an individual soul's intellectual level produces his or her higher consciousness of God.

The soul's mental level centers on our thoughts, based on the recognition of the enduring value to our existence of our ideas and ideals. As developed in Chapter 2, each of us strives to find meaning to our life by understanding our special earthly calling. By living up to this expectation and being who we are supposed to be, we achieve the fulfillment on the physical plane of our existence for which we yearn.

Fourth, each soul embodies a spiritual level consisting, in turn, of two spiritual or transcendental energy fields or levels. In the soul's first, or lower, spiritual level, each individual life experience connects, consciously or unconsciously, with God and the Divine Life Force. Each of us experiences our separate self within the context of a larger whole. We strive to belong to this greater whole—to the soul of the universe, in other words, to God—and to find a context for our existence. We sense that somehow we can transcend our own existence, yet not lose ourselves. This aspect of the soul represents the highest degree of awareness accessible to most humans.

At an even higher spiritual level, sometimes viewed as a transcendent field of light, the soul strives to unite with and merge into God. This higher spiritual level represents the part of the soul that is inseparable from the Eternal. This level constitutes the pure part of the soul.

During a human's lifetime, each of these four invisible and often rather difficult to fathom aspects of a soul are interconnected forming one unified, organic whole without any division. The interaction of these four levels characterizes a human's soul nature, his or her soulfulness.

We may thus view our soul as the power that supplies the body with health and energy. It is the power that gives human life its vigor and strength. It is the power that supplies each heart with its emotions. It is the power that enables us to visualize the invisible and create works of grandeur. It is the power harmonizing all the parts of a human being and coordinating bodily action and expression. The soul is, therefore, the essence of a human being.

The soul in each of us represents the invisible energy emanating from God—the Universal Soul. It is a beam of light from the Ultimate Foundation of Light. It is but an infinitesimal part of the vitality and energy from the huge Reservoir of Infinite Power and Strength. The essence of our being—our soul—comes from and is part of God.

At an individual's death, as discussed in Chapter 6, the soul, after experiencing what Jewish sources describe as the "pangs of the grave" and its attachment to the material world, separates from the physical body. Recall the story in Chapter 1 of what Chaim, Reb Elimelech's friend, experienced at the grave after his death.

Then, the soul's physical, emotional, and intellectual levels, namely, our lifetime of deeds, words, and thoughts, temporarily undergo a process of purification in a realm of torment, Purgatory, as detailed in Chapter 7. These three basic levels are further purified as a departed soul passes through the realm of Lower Paradise. The soul then enters the sublime realm of Upper Paradise, there experiencing Divine Bliss. The stages of the soul's postmortem journey in Lower and Upper Paradise are examined in Chapter 8.

Ultimately, as considered in Chapter 9, a soul enters the Divine Storehouse of the Souls, where souls are housed awaiting their eventual rebirth. Thus, when we talk about reincarnation, we're talking about the soul's journey from one lifetime to the next lifetime. Throughout this journey, the soul's highest spiritual level, our yearning to love and to unite with the Divine, remains in contact with God. Ultimately, each soul unites with God.

Let's begin to take a walk through the world of souls, the domain one enters subsequent to death, a realm of disembodied spirits. We turn first to the dying process and the death moment where an individual undergoes various experiences relating to his or her departure from the earthly world.

CHAPTER FOUR

Separation of the Soul from the Physical Body
Part I: The Process of Dying and the Death Moment

This chapter focuses on the dying process and the death moment. The next two chapters, Chapters 5 and 6, discuss death moment visions and the pangs of the grave. Taken together, these three chapters represent the totality of an individual's experiences related to his or her departure from the physical realm. These various stages constitute a continuum of experience in the time frame prior to, at, and immediately following death. Although discussed separately for the sake of clarity, these stages merge with each other. Each stage takes a variable length of time depending on the individual and the circumstances of his or her death.

THE DYING PROCESS

During the process of dying, the elements of the physical body dissolve and separate during the process of death. The mystical Jewish tradition teaches:

We have [learned] that on the [dreaded] day when man's time comes to depart from the world, four quarters of the world indict him, and punishments rise up from all four quarters, and four elements fall to quarreling and seek to depart each to its own side (Zohar II, 218b).

Although this cryptic passage fails to describe the four elements, the author probably refers to the four essential elements of human existence—earth (or flesh), water (or bodily fluids), fire (or bodily heat), and air (or breath)—as they dissolve and leave the human body. The quarreling may connote the tumultuous and rather upsetting process taking placing in the dying person's inner consciousness.[1]

On a physical level, the process of dying, from my observation, involves a gradual withdrawal and ultimately, a shutting down, of different life functions. Someone very close to death generally is drained of energy. Her body becomes heavy and she encounters difficulty in standing or even moving her limbs. A dying individual often experiences dehydration and feels extremely thirsty, needing ice chips on her face, mouth, and lips to avoid becoming parched. Losing the ability to control bodily fluids, she typically becomes incontinent, her body loses heat and her limbs become cold. Finally, it becomes harder and harder to breath. Inbreaths become shallower and outbreaths longer. Ultimately, her breath stops. The moment of physical death has arrived.

DEATHBED RITUALS IN THE JEWISH TRADITION

In the Jewish tradition, a terminally ill individual may offer prayers and meditate, as well as visualize, what the future might be

---

[1]Simcha Paull Raphael (1994), *Jewish Views of the Afterlife* (Northvale, NJ: Jason Aronson), pp. 295–296, 378–379.

like after death. Let's consider how each of these techniques can offer a dying person tranquility, thereby facilitating the transference of his or her soul into the postdeath realms.

No one special form of Jewish deathbed confession existed in ancient times. The traditional Jewish deathbed confession (*Viddui*) has been in use for about 850 years since the time of the medieval philosopher Nachmanides, who lived from 1194 to 1270 C.E. Once widely known and used, the *Viddui* has fallen into disuse in the twentieth century. Only now is it being reclaimed.

The Deathbed Confessional Prayer is outwardly directed. Based on a sentence in Proverbs, "People who confess and give up their sins will obtain mercy" (Proverbs 28:13), the confessional prayer enables a dying individual to speak directly to and make peace with God. Through the deathbed prayer, one who is dying confesses his or her sins, acknowledges his or her guilt, and expresses feelings of regret for failing to live up to his or her potential or fulfill his or her obligations. In accounting to God for a life that's about to end, he or she asks for and indicates a willingness to receive God's forgiveness.

The Deathbed Confessional Prayer, which follows, can be read by or to a dying person:

Deathbed Confessional (Viddui)

I acknowledge unto You, O Eternal my God and God of my ancestors, that both my cure and my death are in Your hands. May it be Your Will to send me a perfect healing. Yet if my death be fully determined by You, I will in love accept it at Your hand. O may my death be an atonement for all the sins, iniquities, and transgressions of which I have been guilty against You. Grant me the abounding happiness that is treasured up for the righteous. Make known to me the path of life: in Your presence is the fulness of joy; at Your right hand bliss for evermore.

You who are the protector of the bereaved and the helpless watch over my loved ones with whose soul my own is linked. Into Your hand I commit my spirit; redeem it, O Eternal God of truth.[2]

By affirming that life and death are in God's hands, the death-bed confessional serves several purposes. First, it represents an individual's turning from evil. As a petitionary prayer, the confessional asks for something we want. A gravely ill person offers repentance and seeks forgiveness from God.

Second, the deathbed confessional also serves as an affirmative prayer to God: Your will be done, O Eternal.

Third, as developed later in this chapter, a dying person, if possible, should try to settle all previously unresolved emotional issues before his or her demise. By enabling a dying person to focus on major interpersonal relationships and how he or she feels about each, the recitation of the confessional may trigger one final attempt by a gravely ill individual to make amends and achieve a reconciliation with family members and friends.

Fourth, the confessional prayer may also enable a dying individual to explore his or her inner life, namely, feelings about God and the fate of his or her soul, as well as the meaning of his or her life and death. In asking for forgiveness, he or she hopefully also realizes the presence of God's unconditional love for us.

---

[2]Adapted from Dr. Joseph H. Hertz (1985), *The Authorised Daily Prayer Book*, rev. ed. (New York: Bloch), p. 1065. Other versions of the *Viddui* are contained in Anita Diamont (1998), *Saying Kaddish: How to Comfort the Dying, Bury the Dead, and Mourn as a Jew* (New York: Schocken), pp. 42–47. Essays and prayers for the death moment are collected in *Jewish Insights on Death and Mourning*, ed. Jack Riemer (1995), (New York: Schocken), pp. 48–80.

MEDITATIONS

Meditation within the Jewish tradition has existed since Biblical times. Although obscured for most of the twentieth century, during the past decade or so meditation has resurfaced within Judaism.[3]

Meditation facilitates our inner journey and enables us to realize our true and authentic being. The meditation process also assists with the process of our inner cleansing and purification.

Meditation represents the act of shifting our consciousness from external to inner awareness. You do this by going within, quieting your mind, calming and centering your being, and bringing yourself to a still place. In this quiet place in which you can reveal yourself, you can make contact with and listen to God, aligning yourself with the Higher Energy. You attain a space to receive spiritual guidance; a place to commune with the Creator and Sustainer. You connect with your God-like nature, often receiving a new openheartedness.

A guided meditation represents another way of going within. But in this instance, the journey is led by someone else, someone who guides you, with a focused message, to a place where you can have the opportunity to meet with God. Through a guided meditation, you can have questions answered, bring light to shadows, and receive spiritual gifts. A guided meditation thus provides an opening beyond your ordinary state of being. You are afforded the opportunity to experience a deeper and more profound state of being.

In a guided meditation, the guide serves as the facilitator. For a successful guided meditation, the guide-facilitator not only needs to direct the process but also enter into the spirit of the meditation.

---

[3]Avram Davis (1996) provides a helpful introduction to Jewish meditation in *The Way of Flame: A Guide to the Forgotten Mystical Tradition of Jewish Meditation* (San Francisco: HarperSan Francisco).

A meditation (or a guided meditation), as an inward spiritual seeing serves as an instrument of attuning to the Divine Presence at the core of our human nature. We affirm the essential goodness of the human personality and believe that meditation can evoke that Presence. Meditation in the Jewish path means developing a greater intimacy with God in every aspect of our lives.

Dying individuals often find two meditations, the Deathbed Confessional (*Viddui*) and the Guided Angel Meditation, to be of considerable help. A gravely ill individual, who is lucid, can use the *Viddui* prayer as a meditation (or a guided meditation) to aid in the departure of the soul from his or her physical body and the transference of consciousness. According to Jewish sages, the *Viddui* helps clear a path for the soul, our deeper essence, to exit the body. It also facilitates a conscious death at the death moment. The deathbed confessional can also be used as a guided meditation for an unconscious or gravely ill person. Whether as a prayer or a meditation, the confession of sins facilitates the transition of a dying person from the world of the living to the world of souls. It helps usher the soul to the next realm.

Although most Jews in modern times are uncomfortable with the idea of angels, the Biblical and rabbinic literature contain numerous references to various angels—but not the Hollywood variety with halos and wings.[4] In the Torah, the term "angel" generally connotes a messenger. Angels are spiritual forces given human form. An angel stops Abraham from sacrificing Isaac (Genesis 22:11–12). Angels appear on Jacob's ladder (Genesis 28:12). An angel tells Manoach and his wife of the impending miraculous birth of Samson (Judges 13:9–20). These angels represent some of the Bible's non-human messengers.

---

[4]In *Ascending Jacob's Ladder: Jewish Views of Angels, Demons, and Evil Spirits* (1998) (Northvale, NJ: Jason Aronson), Ronald H. Isaacs offers an overview of the Jewish world of angels.

Biblical literature also refers to other, rather strange kinds of angels. For example, the prophet Isaiah describes the seraphim, the burning angels with their wings (Isaiah 6:6). The prophet Ezekiel has a vision of the Divine chariot-throne moved by four rather strange, four-faced, four-winged creatures (Ezekiel 1:4–20).

The rabbinic literature is also filled with references to angels. The Angel of Death, discussed later in Chapter 5, frequently surfaces in rabbinic tales.

In short, angels fill the Jewish tradition. Although portrayed as having a wide range of powers, they usually, but not always, represent spiritual forces for goodness. Angels are sent to help us.

Dying individuals receive comfort from the Guided Guardian Angel Meditation. Surrounded by angels, we feel in the arms of safety as our life ebbs. Loved ones can guide a conscious dying individual through this mediation, twice daily, if possible, for ten to fifteen minutes each time.

Guided Guardian Angel Meditation

Introductory Instructions. The guide should try to create a warm, welcoming atmosphere, an environment of serenity and spaciousness for the journey within. Lower the lights, if possible, in the room. Although difficult in a hospital room, candles can set a mood that enhances meditation.

The guide should ask the dying individual to: close your eyes; sit quietly; calm and relax your body by sitting, reclining or lying down; breathe in and out normally, feeling where the breath flows into and out of the body. Adjust the breathing so that the in and out breaths are the same length, thereby bringing about both a relaxation of the body and an alertness of the mind. (Obviously, you need to vary these instructions depending on the individual's physical condition).

The guide should invoke the Angel Michael—the angel of love and kindness—on your right side. The guide should ask Michael to be with you, because sometimes your own love fails, when you're unkind or judgmental. Ask Michael to please help you to be truly loving and lovable. Ask Michael that you wish to receive an experience of caring and generosity, which will warm you more than you could have ever imagined.

Then, the guide should invoke the Angel Gabriel—the angel representing the strength and courage of God, helping us overcome fear—on your left side. Ask Gabriel to help you overcome your fears related to death and dying. Tell Gabriel that you wish to draw strength and courage from God to overcome the challenges that you face.

The guide should invite Raphael, the angel of healing—the angel who represents the healing power of God—who is behind you, to come into your body, the specific painful area and areas. If it's God's will, tell Raphael that you want to experience a miraculous healing in the physical and spiritual realms.

Imagine the Angel Uriel, the light of God, in front of you. Ask Uriel, who provides insight and understanding that come from outside our own minds, to help you know and understanding what's happening.

Feel the presence of these four angels. Call on each of them. They're there for you.

Finally, imagine the Divine Light above your body which flows through your body. That light is the Shekhinah, the feminine aspect of God. Allow the light to surround you with love and encompass you with a protective inner peace.

Help is all around you.

Concluding Instructions. The guide should offer these instructions. The guide should invite the dying individual to come back to the here and now. The guide should tell the dying individual to: take time to ease yourself back; slowly bring your awareness back into your body; feel yourself back in the room and open your eyes.

VISUALIZATIONS

If asked by a dying person, loved ones could enter into a dialogue, an exploration of his or her beliefs about the afterlife. They may offer a dying individual the opportunity, if desired, to become knowledgeable about the Jewish concept of the afterlife. In addition to using visualizations, a gravely ill person could read (or be read) chapters from this book not only as a map of the afterlife but also to help send the soul on its journey and find its way in other realms.

Visualization can be a powerful goal-setting technique for anyone, even for someone who is terminally ill. Making a mental picture of what you want is often the first step to attaining it. Visualization works best when you imagine a specific, favorable experience. One benefit of visualization is that it forces you to identify what you want to achieve. The clearer the goal, the more reachable it often becomes.

By altering our ordinary perspective of reality, a guided visualization helps a dying person travel on an inner journey to the postdeath realms and freely form his or her own internal images of the afterlife. It also assists him or her explore other realms thereby lessening fears of the unknown.

As with a guided meditation, in a guided visualization, the guide serves as the facilitator. The guide–facilitator needs to direct the process and enter into the spirit of the visualization.

The Guided Spiritual Journey Visualization, which follows, can be used to provide visual (nonverbal) spiritual support for a dying person. Loved ones can guide a conscious, gravely ill individual through this visualization, for ten to fifteen minutes, if possible.

Guided Spiritual Journey Visualization

Introductory Instructions. The guide should try to create a warm, welcoming atmosphere, an environment of serenity and spaciousness for the journey within. Lower the lights, if possible, in the room. Although difficult in a hospital room, candles can set a mood that enhances the visualization.

The guide should ask the dying individual to: close your eyes; sit quietly; calm and relax your body by sitting, reclining or lying down; breathe in and out normally feeling where the breath flows into and out of the body. Adjust the breathing so that the in and out breaths are the same length, thereby bring about both a relaxation of the body and an alertness of the mind. (Obviously, you need to vary these instructions depending on the individual's physical condition.)

The guide should ask the terminally ill individual to: visualize your own death, what you think will happen at the death moment and thereafter. Specifically, the guide should ask the dying individual to: explore the transcendent realms, visualize the image of God, identify with universal, transpersonal Higher Soul, and experience the ultimate destination—union with God. Then the guide should invite the terminally ill person to: visualize the transfer of one's consciousness and the soul's ongoing journey.

The guide should invite the dying person to see how God sends back and immerses you in unconditional, radiant love and compassion.

Concluding Instructions. The guide should offer these instructions. The guide should invite the dying individual to come back to the here and now. The guide should tell the dying individual to: take time to ease yourself back; slowly bring your awareness back into your body; feel yourself back in the room and open your eyes.

Afterwards, the terminally ill person should be encouraged to verbalize, if possible, this visualization. The Spiritual Journey Visualization and the ensuing verbalization will enable loved ones to better provide support for departure of the dying person's soul as it begins the afterlife journey.

THE DEATH MOMENT

In the Jewish tradition, the exact moment of physical death is painless. Death, at least for the "righteous," is effortless. "Like drawing a hair out of milk,"[5] there is no resistance, only blissful peace in death. Even for terminally ill patients, ravaged by pain and suffering, at death they typically manifest a peaceful radiance, a tranquil smile of comfort and quietude. Loved ones often describe their faces as "radiant, peaceful at long last."

However, a gentle death is not universal. For the "wicked," the rabbinic literature, using a variety of metaphors (for instance, "pulling a tangled rope through a narrow opening),"[6] describes the moment of death as a painful experience—a time of considerable agitation. In answering the question, how does the soul of a wicked person depart?, one sage, Rabbi Samuel, stated: "Like a moist and inverted thorn [tearing its way] out of the throat."[7]

For Jews steeped in the mystical tradition, death did not evoke anxiety. Rather, the Jewish mystics saw it as an another phase in the soul's evolution. Death was viewed as a peaceful process transporting an individual from the material world to other realms of disem-

---

[5]*The Midrash on Psalms* 11:6 (1959), trans. William G. Braude (New Haven, CT: Yale University Press).

[6]*Ibid.*

[7]*Midrash Rabbah*, trans. H. Freedman, *Ecclesiastes* VI: 6,1, trans. L. Rabinowitz (London: Soncino, 1939).

bodied consciousness. With an awesome sense of calmness, the pious of old made the transition from earthly life without fear prior to their death.

The following description of the death of the Baal Shem Tov—the founder of the Hasidic movement in Judaism, who lived from 1698 to 1760, popularizing Jewish mysticism and making its concepts accessible to the Jewish masses—continues to serve as an ideal model for dying. Fully accepting death and living with the sense that there was transcendent meaning to life, note the Baal Shem Tov's inner confidence and peace, his control and connectedness with self, others, and God, as well as his love and devotion for others:

When the Baal Shem Tov fell ill shortly before his death, he would not take to his bed. His body grew weak, his voice faint, and he would sit alone in his room meditating. On the eve of [the Jewish holiday of Shavuot], the last evening of his life, his [disciples] were gathered around him and he preached to them about the giving of the Torah. In the morning, he requested that all of them gather together in his room and he taught them how they should care for his body after death. Afterward, he asked for a [prayer book] and said: "I wish to commune yet a while with [the Name, may God be blessed]."

Afterward, they heard him talking to someone and they inquired with whom he was speaking. He replied, "Do you not see the Angel of Death? He always flees from me, but now he has been given permission to come and flaps his wings and is full of joy." Afterward, all the men of the city gathered together to greet him on the holiday and he spoke words of Torah to them. Afterward, he said, "Until now I have treated you with [lovingkindness]. Now you must treat me with [lovingkindness]. [The burial is considered the truest act of [lovingkindness], because there is no repayment.] He gave them a sign that at his death the two clocks in the house would stop.

While he was washing his hands, the large clock stopped and some of the men immediately stood in front of it so that the others should not see it. He said to them, "I am not worried about myself, for I know clearly that I shall go from this door and immediately I shall enter another door." He spoke words of Torah and ordered them to recite the verse—"And let Your graciousness, O Eternal our God, be upon us; establish You also the work of our hands for us. . . ." He lay down and sat up many times and prayed with great devotion, until the syllables of his words could no longer be distinguished. He told them to cover him with blankets and began to shake and tremble as he used to do when he prayed the Silent Prayer. Then little by little he grew quiet. At that moment they saw that the small clock too had stopped. They waited and saw that he had died.[8]

The story of the death of Rabbi Mikhal of Zlotchov—who lived from 1721 to 1786, becoming one of the Baal Shem Tov's most prominent disciples and a spellbinding orator—also illustrates that death represents a calm point of transition from one realm of consciousness to another.

In the last two years before his death, Rabbi Mikhal fell into trances of ecstasy time after time. On these occasions, his face would glow with inner light, and one could see that he clung to the higher life, rather than earthly existence, and that his soul had only to make one small step to pass into it. His children were always careful to rouse him from his ecstasy at the right moment. Once, after the third Sabbath meal, he went to the House of Study as usual, and sang songs of praise. He returned home, entered his room unaccompanied, and began to pace the floor. No one was with him. His daughter, who was passing his door, heard him repeat over and over: "Willingly did Moses die!" Willingly did Moses die!" She was greatly troubled and called one of

---

[8]Adapted from *Jewish Reflections on Death*, ed. Jack Reimer (New York: Schocken, 1974), pp. 26–27.

her brothers. When he entered, he found his father lying on the floor on his back, and heard him whisper the last word of the confession, "One," with his last breath.[9]

The Hasidic rebbes strove to go through death, particularly the death moment, fully conscious and in contact with God. They made the transition from earthly life with calmness and equanimity. They accepted death as a means of affirming life.

ASSISTING THE TERMINALLY ILL PRIOR TO DEATH

Although difficult for nearly all of us to contemplate, according to Jewish sages, we should not fear the process of dying and the death moment. For all pain and suffering we may experience prior to death, the exact moment of death will mark a time of peaceful transition as we embark on the postmortem journey of the soul, affording us incredible possibilities for emotional, intellectual, and spiritual growth.

According to the Jewish tradition, a dying person is to be treated as a living being in all aspects, even if comatose or suffering from mental disabilities, such as senility. Because the moment of death represents the point in time when the soul begins to leave the physical body, strive to go through the death process, as the Baal Shem Tov did, fully lucid.

Allow a terminally ill individual to die in dignity, surrounded by his or her loved ones. A dying person shouldn't, if at all possible,

[9]Martin Buber (1975), *Tales of the Hasidim: The Early Masters*, trans. Olga Marx (New York: Schocken), pp. 156–157.

make the passage unaided. Being with someone when he or she is dying represents an act of lovingkindness, so important from the perspective of Spiritual Judaism.

Beyond being there at the end, the beloved should see that the dying person's physical as well as emotional and spiritual needs are met.

MEETING PHYSICAL NEEDS

Make a gravely ill person as comfortable as possible thereby lessening any unnecessary pain and suffering.[10] Whether an individual dies at home, in a hospice, or a hospital, see that the dying person's physical care needs are met. This may require the continuous presence of family members and friends throughout the day.

Despite Robert and Linda's wishes for their mom, Ruth, an 80-year-old widow, her final months were marked with confusion and often unnecessary pain. She was shuttled from one medical specialist to another, including a surgeon, an oncologist, a radiologist, a cardiologist, and finally, a gastroenterologist. Ruth became frightened and weak.

When she stopped eating, three weeks before her death, Robert and Linda knew the end would soon come. But her doctors seemed almost oblivious, unwilling to accept the inevitability of Ruth's death.

Efforts to prolong Ruth's life, specifically her oncologist's decision to continue chemotherapy, as is too often the case, merely extended the pain of her dying. Her innards battered by chemo, Ruth's pain became so intense that massive doses of morphine couldn't suppress her agony.

As life ebbs for the terminally ill, focus on the use of pain control medication. Make certain that a dying person, such as Ruth, does not experience, if at all possible, severe, uncontrolled pain. Concerns

---

[10]Simcha Steven Paull (1986), *Judaism's Contribution to the Psychology of Death and Dying* (Ph.D. diss., California Institute of Integral Studies), pp. 334–336.

about drug usage, including unreasonable fears about addiction to pain control medication, may cause physicians to underutilize pain medicine. For the terminally ill, these fears are simply ridiculous. They're going to die soon, anyway.

It is paramount that a dying person's pain be adequately controlled and he or she be comfortable. In nearly all situations, this is now medically feasible.[11] Thus, pain control medication should be given as the dying person, if lucid, desires. Otherwise, loved ones must insist on the use of pain control medication.

The utilization of pain control meditation should, however, take into account the reality of the death-moment visions. As detailed in Chapter 5, at or near the death moment, an individual undergoes rather significant, internal, subjective changes. The death-moment visions help a person exit the earthly world and enter the postmortem realms as a disembodied soul. Administer medication to minimize physical pain but allow, if at all possible, a patient to remain conscious, aware, and able to relate to both the objective and his or her own subjective realities as well as his or her objective situation.

In addition to focusing on controlling and managing a dying person's pain, make certain that he or she is comfortable. A limitless number of physical concerns may arise, including difficulties with breathing and bowel movement, nausea and vomiting, as well as sleep disorders. Deal with all of these physical needs. The requisite medical technology and knowledge currently exist to control just about every form of physical distress among the dying.

In addition to addressing a dying individual's physical discomfort, his or her emotional and spiritual quandaries must be dealt with. Provide emotional and spiritual support, if desired by a person whose life is ebbing.

---

[11]A technical analysis of pain control, useful to a layperson, is provided by Cicely M. Saunders and Mary Baines (1989), *Living with Dying: The Management of Terminal Disease*, second ed. (New York: Oxford University Press).

MEETING EMOTIONAL AND SPIRITUAL NEEDS

The ongoing agony experienced by a terminally ill person, often hooked up to tubes and monitors in a sterile hospital room as Ruth was, offers the potential for a beautiful sharing experience. New horizons of emotional and spiritual possibilities for awareness and transcendence exist beyond the outwardly bleak immediate concerns. How much you appreciate life when you're about to lose it. Every extra day of life and breath represents a gift from God.

People diagnosed with a terminal illness often are jolted into a new awareness and mindfulness about their lives. For however brief a period of time, what a teacher their illness is. Stages of end-of-life growth include closure of personal and work-a-day relationships, development of love for self and others, exploration of the meaning of one's life, recognition of a new self beyond one's personal life, the vision of transcendent realms, and the acceptance of the finality of life. The process of dying, life's final chapter, no matter how messy and painful, thus offers the gravely ill opportunities to grow within themselves and with others. Death can be transforming and liberating—emotionally and spiritually.[12]

Many, like Marv, a 51-year-old victim of prostate cancer, ask themselves: Who am I? What is my life about? What have I accomplished in my life? What do I need to express? What's my unfinished business that I need to complete? How am I going to spend the rest of my limited days?

During the last weeks of his life, Marv came to perceive what was genuinely meaningful to him. He was able to let go of what was unimportant. It became a time of a rather remarkable spiritual awakening. Marv never felt so alive as when he was dying.

How can we create this emotionally satisfying, spiritual-oriented environment? A time for reflection, reconciliation, and ultimately, closure.

---

[12]Paull, *Judaism's Contribution*, pp. 336–338.

Try, if at all possible, not to leave a dying person, whether in a hospital, a hospice, or at home, alone and scared. He or she needs to be surrounded by family and friends so that he or she does not feel abandoned or isolated. Rather, provide the warm sun of loving attention.

At the bedside, be present for and learn to listen—to really listen—to the terminally ill person, to what is said (both verbally and non-verbally) and what is unstated, but implied. They should "be there" and "go with the flow." Allow a dying individual to be your guide and bring up whatever he or she wants to talk about or needs to say—thoughts, fears, hopes, regrets, feelings about death and dying, good and bad memories, whatever. It's important to make a dying person feel safe, no matter what he or she reveals.

Ten days before his death, Jack's father, who had had various coronary problems during the previous year, told him, in a melancholy voice of acceptance and inner peace: "I'm ready to go. I'd like to have more time, but, I know it's time." Over the next few days, Jack was able to inquire into his dad's wishes. Jack asked his dad, if he had two more years, free from his illness, "What would you do?" "I would be more loving and kind," his father responded with calm certainty. Just before he settled into a coma, death clarified his desire to be a loving and kind person. He felt and expressed love, the essence of Spiritual Judaism.

In opening your heart to a dying person and offering your full support, always strive to send your unconditional lovingkindness, compassion, and acceptance. Often sitting quietly and holding a hand (or touching the face) is sufficient. Make the dying person feel loved, accepted, and understood.

Following the model of the Baal Shem Tov's departure from life, described earlier in this chapter, transmit a sense of equanimity and a peaceful acceptance of death to a terminally ill person. Try to make him or her understand that, according to the Jewish tradition, death, particularly the moment of death, will be a peaceful, painless experience.

Studies of the near death experience confirm that death serves as a peaceful transition. Near death experiencers report that after being pronounced clinically dead, they typically felt blissful. They experienced what one woman who was resuscitated after a heart attack described as "peace, comfort, ease—just quietness."[13] It's as if they've seen something wonderful. Perhaps, just a second before the soul leaves the body, we understand so much, so deeply.

Do not send "negative" thoughts or feelings, such as fear, guilt, sadness, or attachment. Your optimal attitude and your verbalizations as well as your accompanying actions and emotional expressions should convey an openhearted love for the dying person.[14]

Give the terminally ill permission to die, as Jack did in caring for his dad. Reassure him or her that the survivors will be allright. He or she needn't worry about loved ones.

Offer the dying person the calm certainty of knowing that, according to Jewish tradition, he or she is, and will continue to be, safely held in God's loving arms. In time, his or her soul will, as discussed more fully in this book, experience healing, rebirth, and ultimately be united with God.

Even if the dying person is in a coma, loved ones can communicate through various means, including, touch, eye contact, music, or loving and compassionate thoughts. It's still not too late for them to use their mind and heart in positive ways. Express your regrets, saying, "I'm sorry." Tell a parent or a child, "I love you." Or, to say, "It's OK. You can let go. I'll be allright." The beloved also can express love and compassion through their hearts.

It's also helpful to understand what not to do. Kübler-Ross tells a story of the fear and discomfort loved ones shouldn't convey, reflecting their inability to let go. Little Suzy, who was in a hospital

---

[13]Raymond A. Moody, Jr. (1976), *Life After Life: The Investigation of a Phenomenon—Survival of Bodily Death* (New York: Bantam), p. 37.

[14]Paull, *Judaism's Contribution*, p. 346.

dying of leukemia, was attended by her mom for weeks. Her mother, implicitly or explicitly, conveyed to Suzy: "Honey, don't die on me. I can't live without you." This message only makes individuals, whether young or old, feel guilty. The dying, even very young children, often ask loved ones to leave the hospital. As Suzy put it, "Mommy you seem so tired, why don't you go home and rest. I'm really okay." Mom left. Thirty minutes later the hospital called, expressing regret that her daughter had just passed away.[15]

Often during the dying process, individuals need to engage in "finishing business," cleaning up and healing old, previously unresolved emotional and relationship "baggage."[16] Be particularly sensitive to a dying person's efforts to come to terms with others, communicating previously unexpressed feelings and emotions, such as, guilt, jealousy, greed, anger, desire, or anxiety.

The dying process can serve as a profound time of reconciliation and transformation. Encourage a dying person, if receptive, to make up with family members and friends by addressing failed relationships, old grievances, and hurts inflicted on or by others. By being more openhearted, he or she may be ready to ask forgiveness from others and to offer forgiveness to others as well as to him- or herself.

Illustrative of forgiveness on the Divine level, a folktale is told about the Maggid of Koznitz, Rabbi Israel Hopstein of Koznitz, who lived between 1740 and 1814. The Maggid of Koznitz was a phenomenal Talmudic and kabbalistic scholar and an accomplished preacher. As a healer, his prayers for the sick and the needy, as well as for childless couples, were often answered. Prior to his death, he prayed fervently to God on the eve of Yom Kippur, asking for Di-

---

[15]Adaped from Elisabeth Kübler–Ross (1991), *On Life After Death* (Berkeley, CA: Celestial Arts), p. 52.

[16]Stephen Levine (1982), *Who Dies? An Investigation of Conscious Living and Conscious Dying* (Garden City, NY: Anchor), pp. 73–83.

vine forgiveness. In addition to requesting God's forgiveness, and demanding a definitive reply, he cried out, "Therefore, I ask You; if it has been easy for me to take on myself the burden of the Jewish people and to perform this service the last year during my illness, how burdensome can it be for You to speak two words?" Instantly his being was filled with unimaginable joy as he heard two words descend from on High: "I forgive." Soon afterward he died.[17]

As developed in Chapter 2, although forgiveness represents an important part of Spiritual Judaism, forgiveness is often quite diffi-cult. Each of us continues to fear being hurt or rejected again. We may be unable to let go of our past perceptions. What has been done to us in the past may approach being unforgivable.

One anecdote reveals the guilt that often stays with survivors when the love and forgiveness is held back. Monica waited outside her dying ex-husband's hospital room.[18] For three weeks she main-tained her vigil. She was there to provide support for her grown twin daughters. Although she contemplated it, Monica remained unable to go into her ex-husband's room and forgive him. She could not let go of the anger which seared within her, emanating from the time her ex-husband left her when she was pregnant with the twins and ran off to live with another woman.

As she put it: "He hurt me so much. I simply can't forgive him."

How much better it would have been for Monica and her ex-husband, if she had visited with him, even briefly, before he died.

Monica carries her martyrdom with her. She now recognizes, however, that the incompleteness of her relationship with her late ex-husband has left her with lasting feelings of guilt.

Encouraging an admission of past mistakes and asking for for-

---

[17]Adapted from *The Hasidic Anthology: Tales and Teachings of the Hasidim*, ed. and trans. Louis I. Newman (Northvale, NJ: Jason Aronson, 1987), p. 69.

[18]Adapted from a lecture by Simcha Paull Raphael, "Jewish Views of the Afterlife," May 21, 1997.

giveness is often quite powerful. It opens the possibility of healing
old wounds and tapping, from the viewpoint of Spiritual Judaism,
the power of love. By facilitating reconciliation between estranged
children, parents, siblings, and others, the quest for forgiveness often
enables a terminally ill person to reach closure with and open unconditionally into love and compassion for his or her closest relatives and friends.

I've observed dying individuals reconcile just before death with
estranged parents, children, or siblings. Some of these difficult family situations go back decades (for instance, stubborn siblings who
long ago had a quarrel and hadn't spoken until one of them was
dying).

In contrast to a sudden, unexpected death—a heart attack, a car
accident, or a plane crash—a slowly developing illness with a fatal
outcome, such as cancer or AIDS, gives the survivors time to ask
for forgiveness or a chance to resolve old, unfinished emotional
business. With the AIDS epidemic, parents can do the same thing
with their dying adult children. Fathers, for instance, who previously
rejected a homosexual son can ask for forgiveness to avoid the lifetime burden of guilt that Monica continues to experience.

Kübler-Ross describes a father who hung around the hospital
where his 23-year-old son was dying:

He refused to go in and face him, but he showed up every single day.
One evening, shortly before the end of visiting hours, an orderly no-
ticed him again. He stood behind the father and gently moved him to
the door of his son's room. "Just come in with me and take a glimpse
at him," he said ever so softly, opening the door at the same time. The
father looked, and shocked at the appearance of the skeleton-like figure in the bed, abruptly stated: "This is not my son." A very small voice
came from near the pillow, "Yes, dad, it's me, Richard, your son." The
father hesitated, made a shy step towards his son, and minutes later
their tears mingled as he leaned over his son, saying over and over again,
"I'm sorry, I'm sorry. . . " I have never seen Richard with such a beam-

ing expression on his face. "I knew you would come before it was too late," he said. "Now I can let go and die in peace. . . "[19]

Sometimes anger dissolves within the context of a new vision of the bigger picture of life and death. A 77-year-old widow, Edith, lay dying in a hospital from bone cancer. As ill-tempered and nasty as could be, one old tough "battle axe," Edith had alienated everyone in her life. Her children and grandchildren refused to visit her. Even in the hospital, she continued to be mean to people. The nurses spent as little time as possible with her.

One morning at 2 A.M. she rang for the nurses, but no one came to help her. At that moment, Edith finally threw up her hands and "let go." She learned the lesson of love and forgiveness. Although she died four weeks later, she opened her heart to her children and grandchildren. She became the "Mom" and "Grandma" they had never known before. Edith realized that she didn't have a moment to lose in telling the important people in her life how much she really loved them. Love flowed and with it forgiveness.

Depending on the circumstances of the dying process, there may not be sufficient time or energy for a terminally ill person to personally heal old resentments and fears, either face-to-face or over the telephone. In such a situation, various prayers or meditations may be used to open the heart and enable a gravely ill person to let go of the longstanding resentments that block his or her openheartedness.

The Deathbed Confessional (*Viddui*), as a prayer or meditation, can be used not only to ask for forgiveness from God but also to seek forgiveness from and of other humans. Listening to a deathbed confession, particularly as an expression of interpersonal forgiveness, takes considerable sensitivity. Remember that a terminally ill individual may not want to reveal well-kept secrets, the scars of failed

---

[19]Kübler–Ross, *On Life After Death*, p. 80.

interpersonal relationships, or the hurts inflicted on others that generate feelings of guilt and emotional distress. Provide a safe space for the expression of regrets, fears, or sadness resulting from past deeds, words, or thoughts.

Acting as a guide, loved ones can use the Guided Forgiveness and Lovingkindness Meditation or Visualization to facilitate the process of reconciliation (rather spontaneously experienced by Edith), before someone dies, bringing lasting healing to previously troubled relationships. The guide should take a terminally ill person through this meditation or visualization for ten to fifteen minutes.

Guided Forgiveness and Lovingkindness Meditation—Visualization

Introductory Instructions. The guide should try to create a warm, welcoming atmosphere, an environment of serenity and spaciousness for the journey within. Lower the lights, if possible, in the room. Although difficult in a hospital room, candles can set a mood, enhancing meditation or visualization.

The guide should ask the dying individual to: close your eyes; sit quietly; calm and relax your body by sitting, reclining or lying down; breathe in and out normally, feeling where the breath flows into and out of the body. Adjust the breathing so that the in and out breaths are the same length, thereby bringing about both a relaxation of the body and an alertness of the mind. (Obviously, you need to vary these instructions depending on the individual's physical condition).

The guide should ask the dying individual to feel surrounded by warmth and love. Allow any anger to dissolve into the warmth and love. With each breath, breathe in warmth, feel the warmth nourishing you.

Breathe in love and feel the openness that love creates in you. Allow the warmth and love to give rise to forgiveness. The power of forgiveness is so great.

The guide should ask the dying individual to contemplate forgiveness—its meaning and what it might mean to bring forgiveness into your life.

The guide should ask the dying individual to visualize another person whom you resent. With a new state of openness, invite that person into your heart. Notice whatever blocks their approach to your heart—the problem, the hurt, the fear, the anger, or whatever. Enter into and continue a dialogue with that person, until there's nothing more to say.

Now, try to let that person through to your heart. Let go of the pride that holds on to resentment. Allow the pain of old hurts to dissolve.

In your heart, say I forgive you for whatever you did in the past, whether intentionally or unintentionally, through your deeds, words, or thoughts, that caused me pain or hurt. Repeat the words: I forgive you. Allowing the forgiveness to grow, let go of your resentments and open unconditionally into love and compassion.

Then, repeat this for others whom you resent.

Next, visualize someone who resents you—someone whom you have caused pain. Someone who has put you out of their heart.

In a new state of openness, invite that person into your heart. Notice what blocks their approach to your heart—your fear, your guilt, or whatever. Try to let that person through to your heart.

From the bottom of your heart, ask for their forgiveness: I ask for your forgiveness for what I did in the past, whether intentionally or unintentionally, through my deeds, words, or thoughts, that caused you pain or hurt. Repeat the words: Please forgive me. Again, let yourself be touched by the possibility of forgiveness. Ask him or her to let you back into their heart.

Then, repeat this for others whom you may have hurt.

Let your heart fill with forgiveness and lovingkindness for yourself. Repeat: May I be happy and at peace. May I be free from anger, pain, fear, and doubt. May I be filled with love.

Concluding Instructions. The guide should offer these instructions. The guide should now invite the dying individual to come back to the here and now. The guide should tell the dying individual to: take time to ease yourself back; slowly bring your awareness back into your body; feel yourself back in the room and open your eyes.

By engaging in emotional cleansing and finishing relationship "business" prior to death, both the survivors and a terminally ill individual will, according to the Jewish tradition, as discussed in detail in Chapters 6 and 7, help alleviate the departed soul's suffering in the postdeath realms. The successful resolution and completion of difficult relationships between the dying individuals and his or her family members and friends will also make the process of grief and bereavement significantly easier for the survivors.[20]

Saying our final goodbyes to a family member or a close friend is, of course, difficult for all of us. Be aware of the expected emotional reactions as the last goodbyes are said. We experience great grief at the impending physical separation. Tears come with remembrance and memories. We seem unable to let go. However, the souls

---

[20]Paull, *Judaism's Contribution*, p. 338.

of peaceful living beings can help the soon-to-depart soul overcome its attachment to earthly life and make its transition to the postdeath realms. Let's see how death-moment visions enter into the soul's separation from a dying individual's physical body.

CHAPTER FIVE

Separation of the Soul from the Physical Body
Part II: Death-Moment Visions

According to the Jewish mystical tradition, decedents generally experience four internal, subjective death-moment visions immediately prior to, at, or shortly after the moment of death. This chapter discusses these four visions: seeing the Clear Light, encountering previously deceased relatives and angels, undergoing a life review, and ultimately, passing through a tunnel.

From the perspective of Spiritual Judaism, the life review, which consists of our life passing before our eyes, is especially important. Because our purpose in life centers on loving unconditionally and extending forgiveness, we'll be judged someday by this standard.

This chapter also examines how loved ones can help a terminally-ill person, prior to death, deal with these death-moment visions, thereby deepening the soon-to-depart individual's spiritual path.

DEATH-MOMENT VISIONS

With death imminent, we enjoy the ability to see elements in worlds generally otherwise unavailable to human beings. According to the mystical tradition,

> ... [W]hen a man's [judgment] hour is near, [an angel] commences to call to him, and no one knows [except] the patient himself, as we have [learned], that when a man is ill and his time is approaching to depart from the world, a new spirit enters into him from above, in virtue of which he sees things which he could not see before, and then he departs from the world (Zohar II, 218b).

During the dying process, in addition to the dissolution of the elements of the physical body discussed in Chapter 4, most individuals encounter four visionary experiences: 1) seeing the Clear Light; 2) encountering previously deceased relatives and friends as well as angels; 3) undergoing a life review; and 4) passing through a tunnel.[1] The order in which these internal, subjective visions occur varies from person to person, depending on the circumstances of death and extent of his or her spiritual development. The point is that, even after physical death, the internal process of dissolution continues on a nonphysical level.

Descriptions of near death experiences (NDEs,) as well as NDE studies, corroborate the portrayal of the four death-moment visions we'll see in Jewish texts and tales. NDE literature began nearly twenty-five years ago when Raymond Moody published his celebrated book on NDEs, *Life After Life*.[2] Based on interviews with

---

[1]Simcha Paull Raphael (1994), *Jewish Views of the Afterlife* (Northvale, NJ: Jason Aronson), pp. 132–136, 288–291, 294, 342, 379–380.

[2]Raymond A. Moody, Jr. (1976), *Life After Life: The Investigation of a Phenomenon—Survival of Bodily Death* (New York: Bantam). Near death experiences (NDEs) are also discussed in Michael B. Sabom (1982), *Recollections of Death: A Medical Investi-*

150 people who claimed to have had a NDE, the book offered first-hand accounts of the afterlife. After describing the dying process, most subjects reported going rapidly through a dark tunnel to a point of light many times brighter than anything they'd ever seen, but warm, loving, and accepting. Some reported communications with previously deceased relatives. A few described undergoing a life review consisting of a replay of all of their thoughts, words, and deeds as well as the impact of their existence on others.

EXPERIENCING THE CLEAR LIGHT

During the dying process, or at or immediately after the moment of death, an individual may experience a glimpse of the Clear Light, a beautiful and intense light, much brighter than anything experienced on earth. This is the radiant light of the soul's higher spiritual aspects. It's sometimes described as having been created from the perspiration of angels who sing praises to God. The vision of this light generally occurs at, or soon after, the demise of one's physical body.

Jewish mystical sources describe how, at this time, a departed soul takes a dip in the River of Light and begins to be cleansed from many of the defilements of earthly life. Immersion in the River of Light assists in restoring the soul to its initial radiance. The encoun-

Footnote 2 (*continued*)

gation (New York: Harper and Row)(interviews with 116 persons having a close brush with death, 71 of whom reported a near death experience); and Kenneth Ring (1980), *Life at Death: A Scientific Investigation of the Near–Death Experience* (New York: Coward, McCann & Geoghegan)(study of 102 persons who had a close brush with death). Patrick Glynn (1997), *God: The Evidence: The Reconciliation of Faith and Reason in a Postsecular World* (Rocklin, CA: Forum), pp. 99–137, summarizes the evidence, concluding (p. 136): "It is difficult to analyze this evidence in depth and to come away with any other impression but that science has indeed stumbled on data of the soul."

ter with the River of Light not only helps the dying person leave the physical world but also helps his or her soul become more identified with the spiritual realms.

A dying person may also be blessed with a brief glimpse of God's presence—the feminine aspect of the Divine (the Shekhinah) — appearing as a formless, glowing image. According to the Jewish mystical tradition: "No man dies before he sees the Shekhinah and because of its deep yearning for the Shekhinah, the soul departs in order to greet her" (Zohar III, 88a). Thus, the soul may fleetingly see the radiant image of God's luminescence, and as we are "surrounded by total and absolute unconditional love, understanding, and compassion. . . . we become aware of our potential, of what we could be like, of what we could have lived like."[3]

Whether a soul will notice the radiant Clear Light in one or more of its various forms and not be scared by its majestic intensity, may depend on an individual's spiritual attainment during his or her lifetime. The mystical tradition notes:

> When a man is on the point of leaving this world, his soul suffers many chastisements along with his body before they separate. Nor does the soul actually leave him until the Shekhinah shows herself to him, and then the soul goes out in joy and love to meet the Shekhinah. If he is righteous, he cleaves and attaches himself to her. But if not, then the Shekhinah departs, and the soul is left behind, mourning for its separation from the body, like a cat which is driven away from the fire (Zohar V, 53a).

According to Jewish sages, some "righteous" individuals may recognize the River of Light (representing the upper levels of the soul's inner luminosity) and glory in its radiance. For others, the sight of the River of Light may engender fear. Some may be completely

---

[3]Elizabeth Kübler-Ross (1991), *On Life After Death* (Berkeley, CA: Celestial Arts), p. 61.

unaware of the vision of the Clear Light, which occurs during this phase of the soul's post-death journey.

ENCOUNTERING DECEASED RELATIVES AND ANGELS

During the dying process or at the death moment, according to the Jewish tradition, each of us encounters beloved deceased relatives and close friends as well as angels. The spirits of deceased relatives and friends, those who loved us the most, visit a dying person to offer a welcome and ease the transition from the world of the living to the invisible, post-death world of the souls.

The Jewish mystical tradition describes a deathbed vision of deceased loved ones as follows:

> Rabbi Simeon then said to Rabbi Isaac: Have you seen today the image of your father? For so we have [learned] that at the hour of a man's departure from the world, his father and his relatives gather round him, and he sees them and recognizes them, and likewise all with whom he associated in this world, and they accompany his soul to the place where it is to abide. (Zohar II, 218a).

Numerous near death experiencers report seeing one or more loving relatives who are prepared to assist the individual in making the transition to the world beyond. For the NDEs, however, the beloved tells the person their time to depart has not arrived.

Elizabeth Kübler-Ross recounts the story of a man who witnessed a hit-and-run accident in which a young woman was critically injured. He stopped his car and offered to help her, but the woman calmly told him there was nothing he could do except convey a message to her mother that she was okay and very happy because she was already with her dad. The woman died in the stranger's arms. He was so moved by the experience that he drove 700 miles out of his way to visit the woman's mother. He delivered the daughter's message, only to be told that the woman's father had died of a heart attack about one hour prior to the fatal accident. The young woman had never been informed of her dad's death.[4]

Kübler-Ross also tells about children involved in family car accidents, especially on holiday weekends, such as Memorial Day or Labor Day, who often report that loved ones are waiting for them on the other side. She writes:

> I have made it a task to sit with the critically injured children since they are my specialty. I am aware that they have not been informed that any of their relatives have been killed. I am always impressed that they are aware of those who preceded them in death. I sit with them, watch them silently, perhaps hold their hand. I watch their restlessness, but often, shortly prior to death, a peaceful serenity overtakes them, an ominous sign. It is at this time that I ask them if they are willing and able to share with me what they are experiencing. They share in very similar words, "Everything is all right now. Mommy and Peter are already waiting for me." I am aware that the mother was killed, suddenly, at the scene. But I am not aware that her brother Peter also died. Shortly afterwards, I receive a phone call from the children's hospital that Peter had died ten minutes ago.[5]

The elderly, terminally-ill sometimes ramble and call out incoherently for a departed mother, now dead decades ago, a younger brother, deceased for ten or fifteen years, and perhaps an older sister, who may have died, unknown to him or her, one week ago. A daughter-in law, in retelling her father-in-law's death, described it this way: "It seems to me his dead were calling to him. They were waiting for him."[6]

[4]*Ibid.*, p. 55.

[5]*Ibid.*, p. 54.

[6]Marcia Moskowitz (1995), "Charlie and the Angel of Death" in *Jewish Insights on Death and Mourning*, ed. Jack Riemer (New York: Schocken), p. 43.

In addition to previously deceased relatives and close friends, decedents sometimes encounter angels. An elderly man, Irv, recounted his vision of the guardian angel Michael.[7] Although Irv lived a nonobservant lifestyle all his adult life, while growing up he was educated in a traditional Hasidic yeshiva. In his late eighties, Irv had a serious illness that brought him close to death. When Irv recovered, he reported that the Angel Michael appeared and told him it was not time for him to leave the world. In the mystical tradition, from Irv's long-forgotten Jewish education more than seventy years ago, Michael plays a central role as the guardian of the south side of God's Divine Chariot. Michael also represents the angel of Divine grace, love, and kindness.

In describing various angels, the rabbinic literature refers to a vicious, destroying angel, the Angel of Death, who has the task of taking the soul from the body. One medieval rabbinic interpretation, from the fourteenth century, graphically depicts the Angel of Death, his sword unsheathed, making his presence known before the moment of death, as follows:

> At that moment the man opens his eyes and sees the angel of death, whose length extends from one end of the world to the other; he quakes exceedingly and falls upon his face. From the sole of [the Angel of Death's] foot to the crown of his head he is full of eyes, his clothing is of fire, his covering of fire, he is surrounded by fire, he is all fire. In his hand he carries a fiery blade, from which hangs a bitter drop. This drop causes first death, then decomposition and the lividness of appearances. . . .[8]

---

[7]Adapted from a lecture by Simcha Paull Raphael, "Jewish Views of the Afterlife," May 21, 1997.

[8]"The Formation of the Child" in *The Chronicles of Jerahmeel* XII: 4–5, ed. and trans. M. Gaster (New York: KTAV, 1971), p. 29.

Sometimes the Angel of Death, in more modern garb, appears to the beloved. One caretaker recounts her dream:

> The angel of death appeared to me like someone from a 1930s gangster movie. He wore a trench coat with its collar turned up; his hat covered his eyes so that his face was indiscernible. Like a thief, he was trying to enter our house by prying open one of the windows. Somehow he made it into the house and was walking down the long hallway to the children's bedrooms. I ran out of my room, blocked his path and screamed, "No, not one of us, not the children. Charlie's [her dying father-in-law] waiting for you in the downstairs bedroom. You're supposed to take him, not us. Don't make a mistake!" My screams awakened both Carl [her husband] and me.[9]

A life of good deeds and words—from the viewpoint of Spiritual Judaism, a lifetime of lovingkindness and forgiveness—was viewed by the rabbis as immunizing a departed against the frightening, vengeful Angel of Death. Four protective angels were said to appear and gracefully accompany a "righteous" person out of the world of the living, according to the mystical tradition, thus avoiding the Angel of Death's ruthless actions.

In addition to the Angel of Death, the individual also encounters other angels. When the Angel of Death completes his work, particularly with respect to those aspects of the soul viewed as closer in their essence to the evil inclination, another angel, Dumah, arrives on the scene. Dumah serves as the caretaker for and the guardian of the deceased's soul. In commenting on the collaboration between the Angel of Death and Dumah, the rabbinic teachings note:

> [Once the Angel of Death removes the soul from a person's body] the man dies right away, but his spirit comes out and sits on the tip of the nose until the body begins to decay. As decay sets in, the spirit, weep-

---

[9]Moskowitz, "Charlie and the Angel of Death," p. 44.

ing, cries out to God, saying: "Sovereign of the universe, [where] am I to be taken?" Immediately Dumah takes the spirit and carries it to the courtyard of the dead, to join the other spirits.[10]

The rabbinic and mystical literature also refer to three angels, or in some interpretations, three groups of angels, who appear at the moment of death or soon thereafter. They greet the soul and offer an initiation in the postmortem realms. In commenting on the trio of angels who accompany the decedent's soul, the rabbinic teachings indicate:

> ... [T]he elder Rabbi Hiyya said: When a holy man leaves this world, three companies of angels attend him, one saying Let him come in peace (Isaiah 57:2); another saying Let him rest in his bed (Ibid.); and another walking before him in silence, as the verse concludes walking before him (Ibid.).[11]

Drawing on ancient rabbinic teachings, the writings of the Jewish mystics also describe a catapult used to purify certain souls. Two angels appear after death and toss a soul back and forth from one end of the universe to the other. The catapult purifies the soul from some of the accumulated debris that obscures the higher, spiritual levels of the soul's pure radiance. The catapult helps shake out a soul's extraneous thoughts so that the soul gets closer to its unalloyed essence and attains a measure of inner peace. Immersion of the soul in this cosmic centrifuge further prepares it for its continued journey in the postdeath realms.[12]

---

[10]*The Midrash on Psalms* 11:6, trans. William G. Braude (New Haven, CT: Yale University Press, 1959).

[11]*Pesikta Rabbati* 2:3, trans. William G. Braude (New Haven, CT: Yale University Press, 1968).

[12]Raphael, *Afterlife*, p. 294 and Anne Brener (1993), *Mourning & Mitzvah: A Guided Journal for Walking the Mourner's Path Through Grief to Healing* (Woodstock, VT: Jewish Lights Publishing), p. 197.

Undergoing a Life Review

Jewish sages indicate that each of us also undergoes a review of his or her immediate past life experiences and is held accountable for his or her deeds, words, and thoughts. According to the rabbinic literature, an individual receives an instantaneous, extraordinarily rapid, full color, three-dimensional, panoramic review of all his or her life's thoughts, words, and deeds, both good and bad.

All the details of a person's life experience are revealed. One's entire life occurs at once. He or she knows every thought he or she ever had during earthly life. He or she recalls every word ever spoken and remembers each deed. The rabbis state, according to the Talmud, "At the hour of a departure to his eternal home, all his deeds are enumerated before him, and the angels say to him: 'You did such and such in such and such a place and on such and such a day'" (Ta'anit 11a).

One understands the reasons for and consequences of each of his or her thoughts, words, and actions. Events are put in perspective. We see how our actions impacted others, including strangers. We perceive how everyone's life is intertwined.

Because each of us has angels assigned to maintain records of our good and bad deeds, words, and thoughts, the balance of one's life experience is immediately apparent in the Divine data bank. According to the rabbis:

> . . . [A]ngels are assigned to every human being. And every day they record his deeds, so that everything he does is known to the Holy Blessed One, and everything is put down on his record and marked with a seal. When a man is righteous, his righteousness is recorded; when a man does wrong, his wrongdoing is recorded. Accordingly, when a righteous man arrives at the end of his days, his recording angels precede him into heaven singing his praise. . . . But when a wicked man dies, a man who did not bring himself to turn in repentance to God, the Holy Blessed One, says to him: "Let your soul be blasted in

despair! How many times did I call upon [you] to repent, and [you did] not."[13]

Building on the concept of a past life review contained in the rabbinic literature, coupled with a just reward or retribution for each individual according to his or her actions, words, and thoughts, the mystical tradition describes the life review as follows:

Rabbi Eleazar said: On the day when a man's time arrives to depart from the world. . . . [t]hree messengers [the Angel of Love, who records a person's merits; the Angel of Judgment, who records a person's sins; and the Angel of Mercy, who notes the length of a person's life] stand over him and take an account of his life and of all that he has done in this world, and he admits all with his mouth and signs the account with his hand. . . . the whole account is signed with his hand so that he should be judged in the next world for his actions, former and later, old and new, not one of them is forgotten. . . . (Zohar I, 78b–79a).

Raymond Moody reports on one of the more extended life reviews encountered by a Near Death Experiencer:

When the light appeared, the first thing he said to me was "What do you have to show me that you've done with your life?" or something to this effect. And that's when these flashbacks started. I thought, "Gee, what is going on?" because, all of a sudden, I was back in my early childhood. And from then on, it was like I was walking from the time of my very early life, right up to the present.

It was really strange where it started, too, when I was a little girl, playing down by the creek in our neighborhood, and there were other scenes from about that time—experiences I had had with my sister, and things about neighborhood people, and actual places I had been.

---

[13]*Pesikta Rabbati* 44:8.

And then I was in kindergarten, and I remembered the time when I had this one toy I really liked, and I broke it and cried for a long time. . . .

The things that flashed back came in the order of my life, and they were so vivid. The scenes were just like if you walked outside and saw them, completely three-dimensional, and in color. And they moved. For instance, when I saw myself breaking the toy, I could see all the movements. It wasn't like I was watching it all from my perspective at the time. It was like the little girl was somebody else, in a movie. . . .

Now, I didn't actually see the light as I was going through the flashbacks. He disappeared as soon as he asked me what I had done, and the flashbacks started, and yet I knew that he was there with me the whole time, that carried me back through the flashbacks, because I felt his presence, and because he made comments here and there. He was trying to show me something in each one of these flashbacks. . . .

All through this, he kept stressing the importance of love. The places where he showed it best involved my sister; I have always been very close to her. He showed me some instances where I had been selfish to my sister, but then just as many times where I had really shown love to her and had shared with her. He pointed out to me that I should try to do things for other people, to try my best.[14]

Generally, this instantaneous life review occurs before three members of the Heavenly Tribunal. The life review culminates in the deceased soul signing a confession containing the record shown him or her and acknowledging the justice of the verdict.

We don't blame the Heavenly Tribunal or God for the verdict or our fate. We see what our life could have been like; the potential we had. According to Kübler-Ross:

---

[14]Moody, *Life After Life*, pp. 64–66.

. . . [Y]ou will know that you yourself were your own worst enemy since you are now accusing yourself of having neglected so many opportunities to grow. Now you know that long ago when your house burned down, when your child died, when your husband hurt himself, or when you yourself suffered a heart attack, all fatal blows were merely some of the many possibilities for you to grow: to grow in understanding, to grow in love, to grow in all these things which we still have to learn.[15]

The life review typically occurs at the time of death or shortly thereafter. However, in the case of a slow, lingering death, the life review may take place more slowly. In this situation, the life review may occur over many, many days.

An ethical foundation underpins the Jewish teachings regarding the life review. From the perspective of Spiritual Judaism, we're responsible for our thoughts, words, and deeds during our life. The life review is based on the central ethic of unconditional love and forgiveness. We'll be judged by this standard of love and forgiveness.

Our purpose in life centers on loving and providing selfless service to other humans. Near death experiencers often report being asked the question they found most difficult to answer, "What service have you rendered to others?"

According to the Jewish tradition, good deeds, words, and thoughts result in benevolence after death; conversely, wickedness yields some type of postmortem punishment. The postdeath realms of Purgatory and Paradise are considered in detail in Chapters 7 and 8.

Passing Through a Tunnel

At some point during the dying process, whether at the death-moment or soon thereafter, the soul passes through a tunnel, some

---

[15]Kübler–Ross, *On Life After Death*, p. 18.

sort of a celestial pathway, on its journey from the physical realm to the world beyond. Some near death experiencers recall it as a river, a gate, or a stairway. This tunnel serves as the bridge between life and death. Once the soul goes through the tunnel—a sort of boundary line—death is irreversible. The "silver cord" linking the physical body and the soul is severed (Ecclesiastes 12:6). For Jewish mystics, the soul's postmortem journey begins.

DEALING WITH DEATH-MOMENT VISIONS

When family members and friends visit a dying person who knows (or who wishes to learn) about the Jewish teachings on the afterlife, strive to validate his or her visions and experiences and honor his or her inner, subjective realities. Calmly explain that one or more visions are part of the dying process, thereby alleviating deathbed fears and making it easier for a gravely ill individual to die peacefully. You must, however, continually respect a dying person's wishes and needs.

Specifically, beloved ones can assist an individual facing death deal with: the life review; the encounter with previously departed relatives and friends as well as angels; and the Clear Light.

FACILITATING A LIFE REVIEW

If possible, facilitate a life review to help a dying individual sort through what has gone before, particularly his or her unresolved life experiences, engage in the emotional and spiritual preparation for death, and clear the path for the hereafter. A life review also enables a terminally-ill person to share his or her personal history and legacy with family members and close friends.

Encourage a life review, either in the form of a monologue or a dialogue between loved ones and a gravely ill person, if the dying individual is at all receptive. Facing the inevitability of death may encourage a new openness of communication, an illumination of the past with a new-found love and forgiveness. However, if there's been a past trauma or abuse, from my experience, it's probably best not to force such memories.

The life review can be quite comprehensive encompassing:

Happy moments and sad occasions.

Expression of gratitude and appreciation for goodness and beauty in life, including the experience of love.

Accomplishments and virtues, experiences of growth, and instances of overcoming a limitation or a challenge.

Regrets, grievances, old hurts, unrealized hopes and dreams, undeveloped talents, missed opportunities, failed relationships, and hurts inflicted on or by others.

Important people, whether from a positive or a negative standpoint, in his or her life.

Final expressions of emotions and feelings as well as previously unrevealed family secrets.

Gently, and as sensitively as possible, ask open-ended questions, such as: Is there anything you hold against others (or you think they hold against you)? Can you (and do you want to) bring these matters to a resolution? Although some risk exists that the life review may aggravate a dying individual causing additional and unnecessary pain and suffering, a pattern of a life of worthwhileness and meaningfulness often emerges from these open-ended questions and the accompanying answers. If possible, probe beneath the surface of past words and deeds to the underlying states of mind from which words and acts originated, thereby helping a terminally-ill individual gain a fuller perspective on his or her life.

Edna, on her deathbed, thought her life meaningless. By having her reminisce about her marriage and children, as well as the various community and social organizations she had belonged to, Edna came to see her life as worthwhile. Her anxieties overcome, Edna died at peace.

Loved ones may find the Guided Life Review Meditation and journal exercise useful in facilitating a life review. Entering into the spirit of the meditation, they should guide a dying individual through the meditation for ten to fifteen minutes.

Guided Life Review Meditation

Introductory Instructions. The guide should try to create a warm, welcoming atmosphere, an environment of serenity and spaciousness for the journey within. Lower the lights, if possible, in the room. Although difficult in a hospital room, candles can set a mood that enhances meditation.

The guide should ask the dying individual to: close your eyes; sit quietly, calm and relax your body by sitting, reclining or lying down; breathe in and out normally feeling where the breath flows into and out of the body. Adjust the breathing so that the in and out breaths are the same length, thereby bringing about both a relaxation of the body and an alertness of the mind. (Obviously, you need to vary these instructions depending on the individual's physical condition.)

The guide should invite the dying person to contemplate what you are grateful for, including happy times, good friends, special moments, love and compassion extended to you.

Then, the guide should invite each special person separately to enter the dying person's openheartedness and engage in a dialogue. Invite the saying of separate goodbyes and thanks to each special person.

Next, the guide should invite the terminally-ill person to contemplate moments and memories associated with: fear, frustration, anger, guilt, remorse, or anxiety. These form the unfinished relational business needing closure.

Concluding Instructions. The guide should offer these instructions. The guide should invite the dying individual to come back to the here and now. The guide should tell the dying person to: take time to ease yourself back; slowly bring your awareness back into your body; feel yourself back in the room and open your eyes.

Dying individuals may find it helpful to make notes on their earthly journey—distinct memories and the accompanying states of mind—whether in a journal, on separate pieces of paper, in a visual form, or on an audio- or videotape. This can be a particularly liberating exercise. Leaving a message or tape of love and encouragement often helps survivors surmount their subsequent grief.

Journal Exercise

A loved one, acting as guide, should ask the terminally-ill person to record on paper, in prose, poetry, or in a letter (or notes) to family or friends, visually in the form of pictures, or on an audio- or videotape his or her memories, as well as past states of mind, emotions, and feelings. Regrets, persons harmed, suffering created by words and deeds, unfulfilled hopes and dreams, and unkept promises should be noted.

The life review can be dictated and written down for the dying person if he or she is unable to do so and wishes assistance. The life review can also be audio- or videotaped.

The guide should gently suggest that amends be made to the appropriate people—either personally, face-to-face, over the telephone, or in writing—as best as he or she can. A message of love and hope can be written or dictated.

If desired, the journal, the pieces of paper, or the audio- or video-tape can be saved as a family history memorializing recollections and closely guarded family secrets. Or, the journal and/or scraps of paper can be destroyed by tearing and/or burning. Likewise, the audio- or videotape can be destroyed.

In connection with the life review, loved ones may also want to guide a terminally-ill person through the Guided Forgiveness and Lovingkindness Meditation or Visualization, pages 88–90 in Chapter 4, as a technique to ask for and give forgiveness.

Do not pressure a dying person to engage in an oral or written life review. You can only provide a safe space, which may be difficult in a busy and often intrusive hospital environment, in which a terminally-ill individual can discuss, orally, in writing, or on audio- or videotape, the events and relationships of a lifetime, one-by-one, express what is in his or her heart, and ask for forgiveness for past hurts and harms to and from others.

The earthly life review will also assist a dying person to question and broadly reflect on the meaning not only of his or her life but also of his or her present pain and suffering. This technique may hopefully help him or her achieve an inner peace with all that he or she has been through during life and now as his earthly existence ebbs.

VISUALIZING DECEASED FAMILY MEMBERS, FRIENDS, AND ANGELS

Visualizing contact, now and in the future, with deceased family members and friends as well as angels opens new vistas for exploring the meaning of eternal life and the soul's postmortem journey. If a gravely ill person is receptive, loved ones may guide him or her through the following visualization, for ten to fifteen minutes.

Guided Visualization of Deceased Family Members, Friends and Angels

Introductory Instructions. The guide should try to create a warm, welcoming atmosphere, an environment of serenity and spaciousness for the journey within. Lower the lights, if possible, in the room. Although difficult in a hospital room, candles can set a mood that enhances meditation.

The guide should ask the dying individual to: close your eyes; sit quietly, calm and relax your by sitting, reclining or lying down; breathe in and out normally feeling where the breath flows into and out of the body. Adjust the breathing so that the in and out breaths are the same length, thereby bringing about both a relaxation of the body and an alertness of the mind. (Obviously, you need to vary these instructions depending on the individual's physical condition.)

The guide should ask the terminally-ill person to imagine your guardian angel or another angel, perhaps one of the four angels from the Guided Guardian Angel Meditation, pages 71–73 in Chapter 4.

Inviting communication with this guardian angel (or other angel), the guide should ask: When did the angel come into your life? What is it doing for you now? What will it do in the future?

Focusing on complete relaxation, the guide should invite the guardian angel (or other angel) to describe various stages of the soul's afterlife journey: the death-moment and the immediate postdeath transition, particularly deceased family members and friends who will serve as guides in the postmortem realms.

If appropriate, also invite the guardian angel (or other angel) to describe: Purgatory, Paradise, and the Storehouse of Souls, discussed in Chapters 7, 8, and 9 of this book.

Concluding Instructions. The guide should offer these instructions. The guide should invite the dying individual to come back to the here and now. The guide should tell the dying individual to take time to ease yourself back; slowly bring your awareness back into your body; feel yourself back in the room and open your eyes.

SURRENDERING TO AND ENTERING THE CLEAR LIGHT

Gently urge the dying person to surrender and enter the intense Clear Light appearing at the death moment or immediately thereafter. Following the example of the Baal Shem Tov's death, set forth on pages 76–77 of Chapter 4, encourage a terminally-ill person to: let go of earthly attachments and desires; slowly and consciously exit the material world; and remain open to the Clear Light and the postdeath realms. Facilitate this process when the dying individual is declining physically but prior to the time when death is imminent as characterized by the gradual shutting down of various life functions, previously discussed in Chapter 4. Obviously, the timing of this discussion represents a difficult judgment call, as a terminally-ill person may still have weeks or days left prior to his or her demise.

DETACHING FROM THE BODY

In addition to encouraging a life review, the visualization of previously deceased relatives and friends as well as angels, and the surrender to and entering into the Clear Light, facilitate a dying person's detaching from his or her physical body and the earthly plane. By striving to break the linkage with his or her body, a soon-to-depart person lessens identification with the material dimension of his or her being, as well as the earthly realm, and begins to focus awareness on his or her timeless, immortal soul and its postdeath journey in the world of the souls.[16] Recognizing that our body is not all who we are, the reduced attachment to the physical, materialistic aspects of life assists the soul in leaving the body and opens us to the next stage of our being.

The following guided meditation (or visualization) helps encourage the process of letting go and facilitates identification with the spiritual dimensions of one's inner life. But remember that letting go takes time. Each of us needs time to overcome our attachment to the material world and our physical body. Guide a dying person through this meditation (or visualization) for ten to fifteen minutes.

Guided Bodily Detachment Meditation (or Visualization)

Introductory Instructions. The guide should try to create a warm, welcoming atmosphere, an environment of serenity and spaciousness for the journey within. Lower the lights, if possible, in the room. Although difficult in a hospital room, candles can set a mood that enhances meditation or visualization.

The guide should ask the dying individual to: close your eyes; sit quietly; calm and relax your body by sitting, reclining, or lying down; breathe in and out normally feeling where the breath flows into and out of the body. Adjust the breathing so that the in and out breaths are the same length, thereby bringing about both a relaxation of the body and an alertness of the mind. (Obviously, you need to vary these instructions depending on the individual's physical condition.)

---

[16]Simcha Steven Paull (1986), *Judaism's Contribution to the Psychology of Death and Dying* (Ph.D. diss., California Institute of Integral Studies, 1986), p. 342.

The guide should invite the dying person to feel: your body, the weight of your head; the weight of your arms and hands; the weight of your torso; the weight of your legs and your feet; the pull of gravity on your body.

The guide should ask the dying person to open the heart to subtler and lighter sensations, to the immortal soul.

With each in breath, the guide should invite the dying person to see how it is received by the soul, to feel the contact with the soul; to see how each breath sustains the soul. Then imagine that each breath is your last breath. The connection between your soul and your body is severed.

The guide should continue as follows:

Let your last breath go, forever.

Let go gently and die. Let go of your attachments, your desires, your fears, your thoughts. Let yourself die and go gently into the Clear Light.

See your soul float free from your body.

With an open heart, let go of your identification with your body and all things that hold you back. Let your soul float free. Let yourself die. Let yourself be free from this earthly incarnation.

Open to your soul floating free of your body.

Concluding Instructions. The guide should offer these instructions. The guide should invite the dying individual to come back to the here and now. The guide should tell the dying individual to: take time to ease yourself back; slowly bring your awareness back into your body; feel yourself back in the room and open your eyes.

The life review, the visualization of deceased relatives and friends as well as angels, the entering into the light, and the detachment from the physical body separately (or in combination) help dissolve a dying person's fear of death, provided he or she is receptive. These techniques also lessen the pangs of the grave, the next stage in the postmortem journey, which occurs when an individual's consciousness remains closely identified with his or her physical body.

CHAPTER SIX

Separation of the Soul from the Physical Body
Part III: The Pangs of the Grave

The final stage of the dying process involves the decedent's surrender of his or her attachments to both the physical body and the material world as well as the gradual acceptance of the reality of death. This chapter develops the Jewish tradition's clear expression of the soul's "pangs of the grave" in the days immediately following death (what Reb Elimelech's friend, Chaim, experienced in the tale in Chapter 1), since the consciousness of a departed individual may be confused or still attached to the body, not even aware that it has died.

Jewish postdeath rituals, including the activities of a burial society, the funeral and gravesite services, and the formal mourning process (*Shivah*) are discussed, emphasizing their soul-guiding functions, particularly in assisting the soul to overcome the pangs of the grave. Suggestions and helpful techniques are offered for all spiritual seekers and those wrestling with grief. For those who understand that consciousness transcends bodily death, these soul-guiding techniques add an important, new level of awareness to this period.

THE PANGS OF THE GRAVE

In the anguish of the grave, a soul undergoes a painful ordeal that Jewish sources refer to as the "pangs of the grave." The soul remains close to its physical body, struggling to hold on to life, and only slowly releasing its attachment to the body and the material world.[1]

Rabbi Simcha Bunim of Przysucha—who lived from 1767 to 1827, stressing introspection and self-searching—explained the "pangs of the grave" by using a metaphor. Once, one of the reb's favorite disciples lost his scarf. As he zealously searched everywhere for it, his companions, seeing his plight, laughed at him. "Do not laugh," admonished Reb Bunim. "He is right to treasure a thing which has served him. Just so after death the soul visits the body that has sunk and leans above it."[2]

Unwilling to surrender its attachment to the physical world, the soul, particularly the soul's physical level, which is closely identified with the body and the material realm, experiences considerable torment during the three- to seven-day period immediately after death. The mystical teachings state: "Throughout the seven days the soul goes from his house to his grave, and from his grave to his house, and mourns for the body. . . . It goes and dwells in his house. It sees them all grief-stricken, and it mourns" (Zohar II, 218b–219a).

Thus, a soul with attachments to the physical realm often remains earthbound during this time frame, traveling between the grave holding the physical body and his or her former home, where grieving family members and material possessions are located. The mystical sources suggest that the soul, aware of the family's thoughts and emotions, may try to talk to survivors and also make use of

[1]Simcha Paull Raphael (1994), *Jewish Views of the Afterlife* (Northvale, NJ: Jason Aronson), pp. 139–140, 166–167, 291–294, 344–345, 381–384.

[2]Martin Buber (1948), *Tales of the Hasidim: The Later Masters*, trans. Olga Marx (New York: Schocken), p. 250.

familiar objects. Seeing the weeping of family members, the soul begins to realize there's been a death.

During the three- to seven-day postdeath period, the soul remains close to the physical body and may even try to reenter it. With the body's decomposition and the soul's realization that it no longer has a body to make a shadow or cast a reflection in a mirror, the rabbinic literature indicates that the soul quickly abandons the body and sets out on its postmortem journey:

> Rabbi Abba ben Rabbi Rappai and Rabbi Joshua of Siknin said in the name of Rabbi Levi: For three days [after death] the soul hovers over the body, intending to re-enter it, but as soon as it sees its appearance change, it departs. . . . [3]

Another rabbinic text describes the soul's journey in the immediate postmortem period as follows:

> All the seven days of mourning the soul [goes] forth and [returns] from its (former) home to its sepulchral abode, and from its sepulchral abode to its (former) home. After the seven days of mourning, the body begins to breed worms, and it decays and returns to the dust, as it originally was. . . . The soul goes forth and returns to the place [where] it was given, from heaven, as it is said, "and the soul returns unto God who gave it" (Ecclesiastes 12:7).[4]

According to the Jewish tradition, to facilitate the separation of the soul from the body, Dumah, the guardian angel of the soul of the departed, previously discussed in Chapter 5, asks the soul its name. Dumah is really inquiring: Whose soul is it? By asking the

---

[3]*Midrash Rabbah*, ed. and trans. H. Freedman and Maurice Simon, *Leviticus* 18:1, trans. J. Israelstam (London: Soncino, 1939) 18:1.

[4]*Pirke De Rabbi Eliezer*, trans. Gerald Friedlander, "The Resurrection of the Dead," Chapter XXXIV (New York: Sepher–Hermon, 1965).

soul its name, Dumah helps the soul recollect its essential essence. Remembering one's spiritual identity aids the soul's separation from the material world. This remembrance also helps lessen the soul's battle to leave behind its physical body.[5]

The mystical teachings indicate that many souls do not experience a painless transition out of their physical body, as the soul extricates itself from the body, only gradually yielding the entrapments of the earthly plane. For most of us, the soul's withdrawal or separation from the body results in an emotional, often tormenting upheaval, as explained in the following excerpt from the mystical literature:

> "For love is strong as death" [Song of Songs 8:6]: it is as strong like the parting of the spirit from the body. As we have [learned]: When a man is about to depart from the world and he sees strange things, his spirit moves through every part of his body and goes up and down like someone who sets out to sea without oars who is tossed up and down on the sea without any peace. It goes and asks leave of every part of the body; and its separation is only effected with great violence (Zohar I, 245a).

From the viewpoint of Spiritual Judaism, what we are most attached to in life may result in suffering after death. Thus, the soul of an individual who lived a life too fully focused on the body's physical aspects or its sensual delights, who was attached to the material world, or addicted to nicotine, alcohol, or drugs, experiences, in his or her clinging, a severely difficult time in overcoming the pangs of the grave. This type of person encounters a world of confusion, a realm of painful torment, in seeing his or her body decompose and in severing concerns with earthly matters. However, this tenacious craving, like any addiction, cannot really be satisfied.

---

[5]Raphael, *Afterlife*, pp. 293–294.

For those individuals who refuse, during their life, to relinquish, or at least lessen, their attachments to the physical body and more generally to the material plane (or those who have died violently or suddenly), the souls' separation from the body not only creates much discomfort but also may require a considerably longer time period. The souls of these decedents may remain in the world of confusion for far more than seven days.

Conversely, the period of separation from the physical body is easier and more rapid for certain individuals who have lived a "purer" life. Who, according to the Jewish sages, falls into this category? Those who have avoided various addictions. Also, those who have cultivated the spiritual, nonmaterial dimensions of life—a more balanced earthly existence—not overly identifying with the physical body and the material world. Because in life they have discerned that the sense of self transcends the body and the earthly plane, the pangs of the grave can be lessened or even avoided.

Building on Judaism's ethical stance—as embodied in Spiritual Judaism's emphasis on lovingkindness, compassion, and forgiveness—the Jewish tradition asserts that a life of "good" conduct, words, and thoughts makes it easier for the soul to leave the physical body. For the "righteous," the separation of the soul from the body may not be an overly painful or lengthy task.

POST-DEATH RITUALS IN THE JEWISH TRADITION

The Jewish tradition utilizes three basic institutional techniques, namely, the activities of a burial society, the funeral and gravesite services, and the formal mourning process (*Shivah* in Hebrew), to honor a dead person and provide a mourning process for the bereaved. These customs enable the living to begin to deal with and accept the reality of death and heal their grief. Although each of us grieves in his or her own way, before the survivors can find closure, they must nurture and validate their experiences with the decedent, both during the deceased's life and after his or her death.

JEWISH BURIAL SOCIETY

Out of reverence for the dead, in the Jewish tradition, after physical demise, the body is never left alone. A watcher remains with the body continuously, reciting Psalms, reassuring loved ones that the body is being cared for.

Jewish burial societies (*Hevra Kaddisha* in Hebrew) arose in each European community from the fourteenth century C.E. onward, in response to the need to cope with mass burials in times of crisis, particularly the Black Plague, which decimated a quarter of the European populace.

Members of a Jewish burial society, in a tradition only now being revitalized in the United States, say prayers and psalms for the deceased and prepare the body for burial.[6] They ask God to forgive the deceased's sins and grant the soul of the departed lasting peace. In addition to offering their respect for the deceased, the burial society members ritually wash and purify the body (the *Taharah* ritual in Hebrew), pouring twenty-four quarts of water over it while reciting prayers. The body is then dressed in a linen shroud, an extra-large pair of unbleached pajamas, devoid of knots, bows, or pockets. The idea is that nothing should block the body's return to the earth and that we can't take any material possessions with us.

The shrouded corpse is then placed in its plain pine coffin, devoid of nails, screws, or any other fasteners. Everyone, according to the Jewish tradition, regardless of his or her wealth or status, should be equal in death.

---

[6]Tzvi Rabinowicz (1989), *A Guide to Life: Jewish Laws and Customs of Mourning* (Northvale, NJ: Jason Aronson), pp. 11–12, 28–32; Maurice Lamm (1969), *The Jewish Way in Death and Mourning* (New York: Jonathan David), pp. 6–8; *Jewish Insights on Death and Mourning*, ed. Jack Riemer (New York: Schocken, 1995), pp. 81–107.

At all times, the Jewish tradition treats the body with utmost respect. Thus, the body is not viewed before or at the funeral service. The prohibition against an open coffin avoids any need to cosmeticize or embalm the deceased.

THE FUNERAL

Just prior to the funeral service, according to tradition, the mourners tear their outer garments (the *Keriah* in Hebrew).[7] Today, mourners are often given black ribbons to cut or tear.

Tearing a garment, or its symbolic embodiment, represents the severing of a blood relationship or the ties of marriage. It symbolizes a broken heart. The tearing of cloth jolts the numbness often experienced by mourners and puts them in touch with and assists in releasing deep feelings and emotions they experience in the face of death. They begin to confront the finality of death.

Traditionally, the Jewish funeral service provides a remembrance of the departed.[8] It offers family members and friends an emotional catharsis and another chance to say their final goodbyes. Marking the beginning of the formal mourning process, the funeral helps the bereaved to accept the reality of death and discharge their pent-up feelings of grief and loss. The void in their lives strikes loved ones as never before. The funeral also reaffirms the continuity of life in the face of death.

The funeral service occurs in a community context. Family and friends offer their support for the bereaved, helping them relieve

---

[7]Rabinowicz, *Guide*, pp. 24–27; Lamm, *Jewish Way*, pp. 38–44; Central Conference on American Rabbis, *Rabbi's Manual* (New York: Central Conference of American Rabbis, 1988), p. 249; *Jewish Insights*, pp. 121–124; Anne Brener (1993), *Mourning & Mitzvah: A Guided Journal for Walking the Mourner's Path Through Grief to Healing* (Woodstock, VT: Jewish Lights Publishing), pp. 109–115.

[8]Rabinowicz, *Guide*, pp. 32–44; Lamm, *Jewish Way*, pp. 45–67; *Rabbi's Manual*, pp. 250–251; *Jewish Insights*, pp. 108–121, 124–140.

their grief and loneliness. A gathering of family and friends serves as a source of strength for the mourners. Love and solidarity help enormously.

The traditional, rather simple liturgy consists of the recitation of several psalms, such as Psalm 23, and prayers designed to reaffirm our faith in a just God, even if we cannot fathom the Eternal's ways. In the face of death, the funeral liturgy affirms a vision of hope and a determination to endure. By focusing on the meaning of life, the service often forces the attendees to take stock of their own lives and to strive to live more constructively.

A traditional prayer for the soul (*El Malai Rachamim* in Hebrew) is recited. This prayer calls on God to embrace the soul of the departed under the nurturing wings of the Divine's feminine aspect, the Shekhinah. Family and friends pray that the soul will encounter God's love and compassion on its afterlife journey:

> Compassionate God, Eternal Spirit of the universe, God of forgiveness, mercy, and abounding lovingkindness, pardon his/her transgressions and grant perfect rest in the shadow of Your wings to _____ who has entered eternity. O God of compassion, remember him/her for all the meritorious deeds which he/she did on earth. Open to him/her the gates of righteousness and light, the gates of mercy and grace. Let the departed find refuge in Your eternal presence. Let his/her soul be bound up in the bond of eternal life. God is his/her inheritance. May he/she rest in peace.[9]

Customary burial rituals, notably, the lowering of the coffin into the ground, with family and friends shoveling earth on the sunken coffin in the open grave, provide a stark reminder that a death has occurred. The sound of the earth hitting the pine box resonates very deeply. From my experience, the mourners confront the fact that a

---

[9]Adapted from Dr. Joseph H. Hertz (1985), *The Authorised Daily Prayer Book*, rev. ed. (New York: Bloch), p. 1073.

permanent loss has occurred. Death is real. The departed, now returned to the earth, "from dust to dust," is gone forever. He or she is no longer among the living. The sense of separation and the finality of physical death is most intense.

Before the gravesite service ends, the mourners recite the Burial Kaddish, affirming God's greatness and calling for peace. Then, the service concludes. Family members and friends approach the mourners expressing words of condolence. They form a double line. As the mourners walk in an aisle between the two lines, they are offered words of hope and consolation: "May God comfort you, together with all those who mourn for Zion and Jerusalem."

Together with the funeral, the cemetery service evokes deep grief, yielding the venting of built-up emotions. Tears flow, reflecting sadness, loneliness, and longing.

FORMAL MOURNING PERIOD

Immediately after the funeral, the formal mourning period (*Shivah* in Hebrew) begins and extends for three to seven days, with the longer period, although customary obligations are suspended by the Sabbath and by major Jewish holidays, following traditional Jewish practice.[10] The pangs of the grave, described earlier in this chapter, corresponds to the *Shivah* period in which friends and relatives, as a community, provide emotional and spiritual support for the mourners, thus comforting the bereaved.

Who observes the formal mourning process? *Shivah* is observed for the following family members: parent, spouse, child who lived for thirty or more days, or sibling (including a half-brother or a half-

---

[10]Rabinowicz, *Guide*, pp. 45–54, 81–89; Lamm, *Jewish Way*, pp. 77–146, 175–187; *Rabbi's Manual*, pp. 252–254; *Jewish Insights*, pp. 141–167, 186–198; Rabbi Aaron Levine (1994), *To Comfort The Bereaved: A Guide for Mourners and Those Who Visit Them* (Northvale, NJ: Jason Aronson). The Sabbath nevertheless counts as a full day of *Shivah*.

sister). Generally, it is most proper for the family members to observe *Shivah* together in the deceased's residence; however, this is not mandatory.

The immediate family members who "sit" *Shivah*, according to the Jewish tradition, forgo all worldly activities, devoting all their energies to remembering and mourning the departed. Other family members and friends visit the mourners to offer their condolences. They're there to listen without judgment as the mourners recall special memories of the deceased and gain insight into the meaning of the decedent's life. Prayer services are held twice daily at the house of the mourning except on the Sabbath, when mourners go to the synagogue.

Some of the home traditions and practices during the mourning period include covering mirrors so as to concentrate on mourning, not personal vanity, and to discourage the soul from returning. A special memorial candle burns continuously in the deceased's memory during the *Shivah* period. The memorial candle symbolizes the departed immortal soul.

The immediate family members sit on small chairs (or boxes), symbolizing the mourners' diminished emotional state, and wear slippers or socks, not shoes made of leather, traditionally associated with comfort and vanity.

Males don't shave. Mourners do not cut their hair and avoid the use of cosmetics. These customs symbolize the mourners' disinterest in their own personal comfort or their appearance to others.

The *Shivah* process affirms community and family ties, provides a source of support and comfort to the mourners, relieves the burden of intense loneliness, and begins a period of emotional healing.[11] Family and friends come and extend their love and support. Through one's presence, a visitor indicates: "I'm here because I care about you. I don't want you to be alone."

During the *Shivah* period, the mourners have the opportunity

---

[11]Brener, *Mourning & Mitzvah*, pp. 87–105.

to begin to grieve the deceased's loss and express the gamut of emotions that follow from a loved one's death in an atmosphere of total acceptance. Within a community context, they also receive helpful emotional support from visits by family members and friends, who often engage in animated conversation, telling stories about the departed, sharing memories, and even some good laughs. Surrounded by a supportive community, the mourners, who are reminded that they're not alone, are encouraged to face and begin to gradually accept the reality of death.

For those observing the *Shivah* process, mourning continues for thirty days, beginning on the day of the funeral. During this time frame, known as the *Sheloshim* period in Hebrew, although the mourners leave their homes and slowly rejoin society, according to tradition, they do not cut their hair, get married, or attend festive events or amusements. They continue to reflect on their loss. After the demise of a parent, the withdrawal from joyous social occasions, such as attendance at social dinners and entertainment events, continues for twelve months (in the Hebrew calendar) from the day of death.

Beginning with the day of the funeral and each day thereafter for eleven months, a special memorial prayer, the Mourner's Kaddish, is recited at communal worship services by those who have lost a parent. Those who have lost a child, a spouse, or a sibling say Kaddish for only thirty days. According to Jewish tradition, those for whom we are obligated to say Kaddish and mourn are: parent, child, spouse, or sibling. The significance of the Mourner's Kaddish is discussed in detail on pages 166–171 of Chapter 7.

USING POSTDEATH RITUALS TO FACILITATE THE SOUL'S AFTERLIFE JOURNEY

From the time just before the death moment through burial, and during the entire immediate postdeath mourning period, the soul of the departed needs considerable support and guidance to avoid or, at least, lessen the pangs of the grave. Yet, all too often in contemporary America, the body of a deceased is transported through hospital corridors and elevators amid noise and idle talk and in complete ignorance of the traditional Jewish view that, in the hours after death, the soul is still in the process of leaving the body. Even in a funeral home, the soul of a deceased often receives little attention while consciousness exits the body. However, this is the time when the soul needs all the support and guidance it can get.

Recognizing the interconnectedness of the world of the living and the realm of the departed, survivors can use various soul-guiding techniques as part of customary rituals to help the soul release its attachment to the physical body and enter the postmortem worlds. Let's focus on four rituals: the deathbed confessional (*Viddui*); the activities of the burial society; the funeral and gravesite services; and the formal mourning process.

DEATHBED CONFESSIONAL PRAYER

First, let's take a step back to the Deathbed Confessional Prayer, previously discussed on pages 67–68 of Chapter 4. The *Viddui* (whether used as a prayer or guided meditation for a conscious individual or recited by another for an unconscious person, assists in the departure of the soul and the transference of consciousness. By lessening its attachment to the physical body, the *Viddui* helps the soul leave the material realm, thereby initiating a conscious death (as exemplified by the last hours of the Baal Shem Tov, discussed in Chapter 4). It also facilitates a dying person's transition from the world of the living to the world of souls. I've observed during the dying process, what can best be described as a "quieting," as a person's soul—his or her essence and deeper presence—prepares to depart the physical body.

In the immediate, postdeath period, loved ones should continue to recite the *Viddui* and visualize the soul of the departed leaving the body. In so doing, loved ones help the soul lessen the often tormenting process of the pangs of the grave.

JEWISH BURIAL SOCIETY

When performing the *Taharah* ritual discussed earlier in this chapter, members of a Jewish burial society should genuinely understand the spiritual significance of washing and purifying the body. When Gail does *Taharah*, she noted, "I really feel there is a difference between the body and spirit or soul. . . . We're not just bone and skins. There's a spirit inside of us; there's a soul and it's always made clear to me then."[12]

Members of a Jewish burial society should focus their prayers and psalms on bringing their consciousness and the soul of the departed into alignment.[13] In this way, the prayers and psalms will comfort the soul, helping it leave the physical body and enter the postmortem worlds.

Survivors may also want to continue the vigil they maintained prior to a loved one's demise for several more hours. Attuning their thoughts to the departed, they can help the soul become free from the pangs of the grave and find its way in the afterlife.

FUNERAL AND GRAVESITE SERVICES

The funeral and gravesite services provide another means for facilitating the soul's postmortem experiences.[14] The funeral service,

---

[12]Caryle Murphy, "A Community Reasserts Religious Values in Funeral Ritual," *Washington Post*, February 15, 1998, B1, B13 (quoting Gail Schwartz).

[13]Simcha Steven Paull (1986), *Judaism's Contribution to the Psychology of Death and Dying* (Ph.D. diss., California Institute of Integral Studies), p. 350.

[14]*Ibid.*, pp. 356–357; Stephen Levine (1982), *Who Dies? An Investigation of Conscious Living and Conscious Dying* (Garden City, NY: Anchor), pp. 202–225.

particularly the eulogy, in which the deceased is remembered in a favorable manner, thereby evoking tears for the loss experienced by the mourners, should remind the soul that it is no longer among the living on the earthly plane. The service should encourage the soul to continue on its journey and not cling to the physical body or material world. In that the soul's earthly work is done, it should be encouraged to move forward, openly exploring all that it encounters as a disembodied state of consciousness.

The funeral service should also seek to strengthen the bonds of healing and facilitate forgiveness between the survivors and the soul of the departed, topics which we will return to later in this chapter and in the next chapter. From the perspective of Spiritual Judaism, time should be made for those present to meditate on forgiving the deceased or asking for forgiveness, particularly, as is often the case, if those present have unresolved feelings and emotions regarding the departed. Loved ones can ask for or communicate forgiveness, as appropriate.

To further assist the soul on its postmortem journey, the funeral service should provide one or more silent periods for those present to align their consciousness with the soul of the departed. Asking everyone present at the funeral to recall, either silently or out loud, favorable, loving memories of the deceased and to convey feelings of lovingkindness and compassion to the soul of the departed assists the soul in separating from its physical body and recognizing that it is no longer part of the material world.

At the gravesite, the living should again attune their thoughts, urging the soul of the deceased to continue on its postmortem journey. They should exhort the soul to leave behind its attachment to the earthly plane. Relying on the mystical tradition, the survivors also should describe to the soul the realms it will encounter in a disembodied state of consciousness: Purgatory, Paradise, and the Storehouse of the Souls, as developed in Chapters 7, 8, and 9 of this book.

FORMAL MOURNING PERIOD

Although often viewed as a social occasion, an opportunity for an ongoing cocktail party, marked by food, drink, and insipid talk, the formal mourning period affords an excellent opportunity for soul guiding.[15] During *Shivah*, set aside time for silent individual (or group) prayers and meditations. Through quiet inwardness, through prayer and meditation, strive to connect with the soul of the departed, sending it affection, compassion, and forgiveness during a period when that soul may be confused, uncertain of its state or whereabouts. Mourners often find the Forgiveness and Lovingkindness Meditation, set out later in this chapter on pages 142–143, useful in offering the soul their love and support.

As a mourner, try to connect, in a personal, spontaneous, and unstructured manner, with the soul of the deceased and to communicate previously unexpressed and, in some instances, unresolved emotions. Pouring out the feelings that you as a survivor hold in your own heart is of value for both you and the soul. You are aided in giving up your attachment to the deceased.

Again, as at the burial service, align your thoughts and consciousness with the soul of the departed, helping it finish its business with this world and speeding it on its postmortem journey. Encourage the departed to leave the physical world behind and open up to the unknown reality the soul encounters as a disembodied state of consciousness.

SUGGESTIONS FOR SPIRITUAL SEEKERS AND OTHERS WRESTLING WITH GRIEF

It's a time of great shock as the bereaved struggle with their grief and become fully aware of their intense loss. I can tell you. Death

---

[15]Paull, *Judaism's Contribution*, pp. 362–364.

of a loved one is like an amputation. You lose a part of yourself. There are few experiences more difficult or unpleasant than the grief following the death of a beloved. The grief burns its way right to your heart. You feel that your heart has been torn in two. You're at the bottom of a well of despair and longing. It's deeply painful and quite bewildering.

If you find that ritual blocks your spiritual life, bereaved spiritual seekers and others wrestling with grief can engage in a number of practices designed to: begin to overcome the shock, heal the grief, and accept the searing reality of death;[16] help the soul detach from its physical body; and interconnect the soul of the departed and the world of the living. Through the immediate postmortem period, it's important for the living to remember the deceased is much more than his or her physical body. He or she has a soul and it's left the earthly plane (or is about to). Let's again consider three time frames: first, the period from death to the funeral (or memorial) service; second, at the funeral (or memorial) and burial services; and third, the ensuing mourning period. Remember that the length and style of mourning represents a very personal decision.

FROM DEATH TO THE FUNERAL SERVICE

From the time of death until the funeral service (a service held in the presence of the body) or memorial service (a service held after the body has been removed), give the soul of the departed the maximum amount of support you possibly can, thereby lessening its attachment to the material world (what the Jewish tradition calls the pangs of the grave), and assisting its entrance into the postdeath

---

[16]Judy Tatelbaum (1980) in *The Courage to Grieve* (New York: Lippincott & Cromwell) provides a good introduction to grief work as does David A. Crenshaw and William Van Ornum (1990) in *Bereavement: Counseling the Grieving Throughout the Life Cycle* (New York: Continuum).

realms. Let the soul receive your thoughtful attention and assistance as the last remnants of consciousness leave the physical body.

Consider, if possible, staying with the body for a few hours after death. Some hospitals and hospices will cooperate if it's prearranged. Continue to pay your last respects and allow tears to flow. Although the body becomes cold and the skin color gradually pales, the deceased's facial expression, even after a painful and prolonged dying process, softens, often quite markedly. His or her inner peace becomes apparent, silently radiating: "Things are O.K." This period of time with the departed often helps survivors begin to adjust to their loss.

Recognize that your thoughts, words, and practices can help the soul of a departed in a number of positive ways. Through prayer and meditation, urge the soul to let go and move onward, now that its earthly work is complete. Coming from the heart, telling the soul, "Go onward," also offers the possibility of beginning to heal your grief.

During this crucial period, express only your most genuine love and compassion for the deceased. Realizing that the soul may attempt to return home, avoid grasping for and quarreling over the deceased's material possessions.

For many bereaved, it's still much too soon to focus on forgiveness. They're in the midst of the initial shock and the accompanying numbness, disbelief, and grief.

Although focusing on accepting the reality of death, a few can begin to ask the deceased to forgive any hurt they caused him or her. These loved ones can start to contemplate any unresolved feelings and emotions regarding the deceased. In asking for forgiveness for issues not worked out and difficulties never confronted in their relationships, they can use the Forgiveness and Lovingkindness Meditation to facilitate the postdeath process of forgiveness and reconciliation, whether in the immediate postmortem hours, or in days or weeks thereafter. Engage in this unguided meditation twice daily for ten to fifteen minutes at a time. Gradually, more and more mourners can use this meditation.

Forgiveness and Lovingkindness Meditation

Introductory Instructions. Create a warm, welcoming atmosphere, an environment of serenity and spaciousness for the journey within. Lower the lights in your room.

Close your eyes, sit quietly, calm and relax your body, breathe in and out normally feeling where your breath flows into and out of your body. Adjust your breathing so that the in and out breaths are of the same length.

Feel yourself surrounded by warmth and love. Allow any anger to dissolve into the warmth. Feel the warmth nourishing you.

Breathe in love and feel the openness that love creates in you. Allow the warmth and love to give rise to forgiveness. The power of forgiveness is so very great.

Visualize the deceased. Within a new state of openness, invite the deceased into your heart. Try to let the deceased through to your heart. Notice what blocks his/her approach to your heart.

From the bottom of your heart, ask for his/her forgiveness: say I ask for your forgiveness for what I did in the past, whether intentionally or unintentionally, through my deeds, words, or thoughts, that caused you pain or hurt. Repeat the words: Please forgive me. Again, let yourself be touched by the possibility of forgiveness. Ask the deceased to let you back into his/her heart.

Let your heart fill with forgiveness and lovingkindness for yourself. May I be happy and at peace. May I be free from anger, pain, fear, and doubt. May I be filled with love.

Concluding Instructions. Now come back to the here and now. Take time to ease yourself back. Slowly bring your awareness back into your body. Feel yourself back in the room and open your eyes.

AT THE FUNERAL (OR MEMORIAL) SERVICE

At the funeral (or memorial) service open your heart to the grief you, as a bereaved, feel in the midst of expressing your pain, loss, and loneliness. It is important to express these emotions and not repress this grief. Continue to send your love and good thoughts to the departed. Begin to let go of your attachment to the deceased but to let go with love.

The beloved have an opportunity to attune their consciousness to the deceased's consciousness. Realizing that we're not just a physical body, remind yourself there's so much more to life and to "living."

Try to connect with and direct your thoughts to the soul of the departed. Through expressions of love and forgiveness, invite the soul to float freely on its postmortem journey and not cling to the physical body left behind.

As Joyce walked away from the grave of her mother, who committed suicide, she was caught in a dilemma. As she begged her mom not to leave her, Joyce asked, "Why did my mother leave me?" Joyce felt guilty as she reflected on missed opportunities for connecting or for patching up misunderstandings. Yet, at the same time, aware of the mystical Jewish tradition, Joyce wished her mother a good and gentle journey.

Although it's difficult for most bereaved to forgive this soon, through the Forgiveness and Lovingkindness Meditation, on page 142, or an unstructured prayer from the heart, loved ones can begin to heal their unfinished relationship "baggage" with the departed.

A memorial service that focuses on the decedent's life and values rather than on the departed's physical body may provide spiritual seekers with a more positive atmosphere for pursuing these soul-guiding techniques.

FORMAL MOURNING PERIOD

In the mourning period include time for spontaneous, individual prayers from the heart, silent meditations, and visualizations. Using these techniques daily, if possible, will assist the bereaved to connect personally with the soul of the departed by sending it love, support, and forgiveness and to communicate previously unexpressed feelings and emotions. Strive to help the soul complete its business with this realm, let go of its attachments to the earthly plane, leave its physical body, and begin its journey through the postmortem worlds. It's also an opportunity for survivors to go within, reflecting on and acknowledging their own impermanence.

You may want to open your heart to God using the practice of the Breslov Hasidim, the followers of Rabbi Nachman of Breslov, the great-grandson of the Baal Shem Tov, who lived from 1772 to 1810. The Breslovers go outside and practice a private prayer, *hitbodidut* in Hebrew.[17] They scream to God, often for an hour at a time. You can do this at home, while driving in your car, or anyplace where you're alone and can shout above your normal voice.

Open your heart to God. Ask the Eternal God from the bottom of your heart: "Please help me." Use your everyday language, not the liturgy of prayer. Express what's in your heart. Tell it to God.

Pour out your feelings to the Supreme Sovereign. Say: "Please

---

[17]Rabbi Nathan of Breslov (1983), *Rabbi Nachman: Advice*, trans. Avraham Greenbaum (Brooklyn, NY: The Breslov Research Institute), pp. 80–87; Chaim Kramer (1989), *Crossing the Narrow Bridge: A Practical Guide to Rebbe Nachman's Teachings*, ed. Moshe Mykoff (New York: Breslov Research Institute), pp. 137–165.

open and heal my heart." Express: your grief, your pain, your sadness, your numbness, your loneliness, your helplessness, your disbelief, your guilt, your confusion, your despair, your resentment, or your inability to make sense of things. Ask for God's help from the bottom of your heart. Let your tears flow. Get your anger with God off your chest.

Visualize God responding, sending rays of light filling you with love and compassion, transforming your suffering bringing you unconditional acceptance and love. Remember, from the perspective of Spiritual Judaism, God loves you. You'll feel the Divine Presence even in the midst of your seemingly unbearable grief and loneliness.

You may want to recite a special prayer, such as the traditional prayer for the soul set out on page 132, to help you, in a more structured manner, visualize the outpouring of the Eternal's love and compassion for the soul of the departed.

Opening your heart to God or reciting a prayer for the soul helps you give up your attachment to the deceased and assists the disembodied soul in its time of transition. Gradually, your longing for the departed will lessen. You'll be less likely to say, "I can't live without you." Letting go of your attachment, you'll come to say, "I wish you well on your journey." This, of course, generally takes more than one week for most of us.

Also consider selecting and reciting (or playing) favorite spiritual teachings, poems, or songs, whether theirs or the deceased's, to help say goodbye and let go. This technique not only helps loved ones begin to accept the reality of death, it may also assist in easing the passage of the soul.

To facilitate the process of letting go and sending the soul on, put a photo of the departed on a table near you. Carve out a special time each day and, for ten or fifteen minutes, sit with your loved one. Tell your loved one to let go of any attachments to the earthly realm and continue on his or her journey.

This can also be a time for the living to open a window of communication with the soul of the departed, building a new relationship that doesn't rely on a physical, earthly presence. The following dialogue between Roberta and her stepson, Mark, who died in an accident involving his car and a school bus, shows that the human relationships continue after physical death:

Mark: Roberta . . . Roberta . . .

Roberta: Oh, Mark, I'm so mad at you.

M: Why?

R: You're dead and I'll never be able to talk to you again.

M: But you are.

R: Oh my God! Mark, is that you?

M: How are you?

R: Are you kidding! I'm miserable! I can't believe this is happening! My God, Mark is dead. Oh my God.

M: I'm alright.

R: Mark, is it really you?

M: Yeah, it's me.

R: Oh my God. Why did you die? How could you do that? I'm so mad at you! You're so stupid! I told you to drive carefully. But no, you always knew better. . . . I could just kill you. You're so stupid. Oh, God, and now I'll never see you again . . . Why do other kids get another chance but you don't? Just one mistake and now you're gone. Oh, what am I gonna do?

M: I'm ok. . . . I'm alright.

R: I hate this! I hate this!! Kids aren't supposed to die before their parents. That's not the right way! It's not supposed to happen that way!

M: It was an accident.

R: What do you mean it was an accident? Mark, doesn't
      God control everything? You know, His will—His provi-
      dence?

M: It was an accident.

R: What do you mean?

M: I mean accidents. Things just happen.

R: You mean they just happen? It's just happening? There's
      no plan.

M: It's just happening . . . Whatever happens is the plan.

R: No, no, no! I need to appeal to a higher court or some-
      thing. This isn't supposed to happen. Isn't there some-
      place I can go to roll back time so we can do it again . . .
      so this doesn't happen? Oh, Mark! Mark! What was it
      like when you died? Please tell me. I have to know. Don't
      lie to me. I want to know if it hurts.

M: It didn't hurt. I was driving down the street. There was
      music on the radio. Jane was in the front seat. We were
      all talking. I looked away for a second and when I looked
      up, all I saw was a wall. I didn't even know what it was. I
      was surprised. I don't remember thinking anything. It
      only lasted a second. Then it was totally dark. And totally
      quiet. It was really dark . . . you really couldn't see your
      hand in front of you. I was wondering if I had my eyes
      open. I didn't feel anything. Then I heard a voice. It said,
      "Well, are you ready?" I had no idea what he meant . . .
      but he sounded nice. I wasn't afraid. I said, "Yeah, I guess
      so." And then things started moving. It was still totally
      dark—black totally, but moving. I could feel the sensation
      of moving very fast through a black tunnel . . . and
      then . . .

R: Oh Mark! That was wonderful. You didn't feel anything at all!

M: No, nothing at all. How's everybody else? They're hurt, aren't they?

R: Yes, but they're mostly upset about you.

M: But I'm ok!

R: I know that—and you know that, but they don't know that . . . and sometimes I don't know that too.

M: You'll be alright.

R: But I can't touch you, and I can't see you.

M: It's different, but we can still talk.

R: But it's not the same.[18]

The mourning process, whether from a ritualistic or a more spiritually-oriented viewpoint, hopefully assists the soul of the departed detach from and leave behind the material world, thereby minimizing the pangs of the grave. Helped by the Jewish perspective on the map of the afterlife, family members and friends can perform an invaluable spiritual function for the soul in the immediate postdeath period.

For some, a time of intense grief also represents an opportunity to get in contact with places within them, otherwise inaccessible. They touch something essential in their own being. They realize there's no place to hide. Their grief sometimes turns their lives around. For the rest of their lives, they open their hearts to others and become more loving, compassionate, and forgiving.

[18]Roberta Ayers Carson (1988), *Mark, My Words: An After Death Dialogue* (Winter Springs, FL: Lifestream Associates).

One other point is noteworthy. Burial has been, and continues to be, the time-honored way to dispose of the Jewish dead.[19] Burial reflects the notion that we're God's creation and that each human being consists of a mixture of body and soul. Thus, cremation, destroying the body by fire, was and continues to be viewed by the Jewish tradition as violating the person. The body should continue to be treated with respect even after the soul departs.

In the nineteenth and twentieth centuries, the practice of cremation, in a closed oven, spread for a number of reasons, included reduced funeral expenses. There's no coffin or gravesite to buy.

With the Nazi's use of crematoria to kill Jews during World War II, a trend away from cremation has occurred among Jews over the past fifty years. Cremation revives thoughts of the horrible time when Jews were treated as worthless.

Although certain Eastern religious traditions view cremation as expunging impurities, liberating the spirit, and preparing and purifying the soul for a better rebirth, spiritual seekers, at least the Jewish mystical traditional suggests, should be concerned about cremation. Why? For most decedents, the soul needs a period of time, generally three to seven days (or even longer for individuals who have died violently or suddenly) to deal with the pangs of the grave. The uncertainty of determining when a soul has actually left the physical body may explain the traditional view that cremation should be avoided.

Jewish sages proclaim that when the soul of a deceased person sees the bereaved mourning his or her passing from the world, the

[19]Rabinowicz, *Guide*, pp. 15–17; Lamm, *Jewish Way*, pp. 56–57. Reform Judaism discourages cremation, "if possible, especially in our generation which has seen the murderous dispatch of millions of our people by way of crematoria." *Rabbi's Manual*, p. 248.

reality of physical death becomes apparent to the soul, who realizes that it is not among the living. Accepting the reality of death, the soul now can give up its longings for the material world and life in a physical body.

Eventually, the pangs of the grave abate and the soul surrenders to the reality of death, entering the next stage on its unfolding postmortem journey. Let's see how the soul returns to its original purity by undergoing various cleansing experiences.

CHAPTER SEVEN

PURIFICATION OF THE SOUL
IN PURGATORY

After death, the soul separates from the physical body, which begins its physical decomposition. The soul passes through various stages on its postdeath journey, experiencing the torments of Purgatory and the bliss of Paradise.

In this chapter, we'll explore the purification experienced by the soul in Purgatory, a state of consciousness reflecting the quality of the life just lived. We'll also examine one specific ritual in the Jewish tradition, namely, the Mourner's Kaddish, which, among other functions, facilitates the soul's cleansing in Purgatory. Because of the importance of forgiveness in Spiritual Judaism, the Kaddish process represents a time for the living to gain a sense of completion with the deceased and, in some instances, to heal a previously troubled relationship. Suggestions are also provided for bereaved spiritual seekers and others wrestling with grief who wish to form a bridge to the realm beyond and strengthen the ongoing avenue of communication between the living and the departed.

THE SOUL'S PURIFICATION IN
PURGATORY: AN OVERVIEW

The soul, after surrendering any attachment to the physical body, undergoes a process of purification in Purgatory (*Gehenna* in Hebrew). Variously described by Jewish sources, the process of purgation consists of a healing transformation in which the soul's defilements and impurities are further cleansed. For some souls, the journey through Purgatory will be very difficult; for others, it represents a far less painful experience. Each experience in Purgatory not only reflects the soul's immediate past life behavior, words, and thoughts but also the depth and nature of the soul's unresolved emotional and relationship issues.

During the process of purification in Purgatory, each soul atones for its earthly wrongdoings. Various impurities of the soul are cleansed, including harmful actions and unkind words, destructive thoughts, harmful attitudes, and negative emotions: hate, aggression, anger, fear, hostility, shame, guilt, anxiety, grasping, greed, pride, jealousy, lust, manipulation, revenge, blame, desire, sadness, resentment, fault finding, and an inability to forgive.

This period of inner dissolution in Purgatory marks the beginning of the end of the soul's desires, attachments, and fears as well as its selfishness and greed. During its journey through Purgatory, each soul discovers a deeper sense of inner peace, love, compassion, and forgiveness.

The graphic descriptions of Purgatory set forth over the millennia in the Jewish tradition make it possible for us, even with our limited minds restricted as they are to our material world, to perceive what we otherwise would likely find difficult to grasp. Thus, view the following descriptions of Purgatory and the processes occurring there as metaphors for the purification through which the soul is tempered and transformed. In other words, the descriptions of a soul's torment in Purgatory are best regarded as a symbolic representation of the soul's state of consciousness or awareness, not as a physical locale or an actual place.

Let's take up the topic of Purgatory in the Jewish tradition historically.[1] We'll begin with the biblical concept of *Sheol*, move on to Purgatory in the rabbinic teachings, and then focus on the graphic descriptions of Purgatory in medieval Jewish literature. This section concludes with a discussion of the period of time a soul spends in Purgatory and the metaphoric elements of Purgatory as described by Jewish sages.

BIBLICAL CONCEPT OF *SHEOL*

Jewish sources initially perceived the place of purification as an actual, physical realm. In describing Purgatory, the Jewish tradition builds on the Biblical notion of *Sheol* as a realm beneath the earth, where the dead "go down" and reside. Portraying the underworld abode of the dead, the legendary Jacob says to Reuben, "If any harm comes to [Benjamin] on the journey you are to undertake, you would send me down to *Sheol* with my white head bowed in grief" (Gen-

---

[1] I have drawn from Simcha Paull Raphael (1994), *Jewish Views of the Afterlife* (Northvale, NJ: Jason Aronson), pp. 51–64, 140–149, 173–184, 264–266, 298–308, and 384–388, who, based on his reading of Nahmanides, a medieval Jewish philosopher (1194–1270 c.e.), develops a view of Purgatory from a psychological vantage point. Various concepts of Purgatory are also presented in Yonassan Gershom (1992), *Beyond the Ashes: Cases of Reincarnation From the Holocaust* (Virginia Beach, VA: A.R.E. Press), pp. 67–68; Anne Brener (1993), *Mourning & Mitzvah: A Guided Journal for Walking the Mourner's Path Through Grief to Healing* (Woodstock, VT: Jewish Lights Publishing), pp. 198–199; Gershon Winkler (1982), *The Soul of the Matter: A Psychological and Philosophical Study of the Jewish Perspective on the Odyssey of the Human Soul Before, During, and After "Life"* (New York: The Judaica Press), pp. 19–20; Rifat Sonsino and Daniel B. Syme (1990), *What Happens After I Die? Jewish Views of Life After Death* (New York: UAHC Press, 1990), pp. 14–19, 26–28.

esis 42:38). The subterranean imagery of *Sheol* is subsequently described more vividly by the prophet Isaiah: "Your magnificence has been flung down to *Sheol* . . . underneath a bed of maggots and over you a blanket of worms" (Isaiah 14:11).

Sheol was seen as a rather bleak subterranean realm: a land of disorder (Job 10:22), as below the sea (Job 26:5), without light (Job 10:21), and enclosed by gates (Isaiah 38:10, Psalms 9:14, Job 38:17). *Sheol* was also characterized as a land of forgetfulness (Psalms 88:12) and a realm of silence (Psalms 94:17 and 115:17), where the dead could not reach out to God (Isaiah 38:18, Psalms 6:6). Weak, powerless ones—in modern terms, ghosts—were said to inhabit *Sheol* (Isaiah 26:14, Psalms 88:5, Proverbs 21:16).

Human existence continued in *Sheol,* but in a weakened, devitalized condition, with decedents assuming shadowy figures of their former selves. However, reflecting a belief in the interconnectedness between the realm of the dead and the world of the living, those in *Sheol* continued to possess, at least to a limited degree, the ability to interact with humans through their knowledge and power. For example, facing a military challenge, King Saul sought the guidance of the deceased prophet Samuel in *Sheol* (I Samuel 28:12–20).

Initially, *Sheol* was seen as an amoral realm removed from God's care and control. The punitive aspects that subsequently came to characterize *Sheol* were lacking. Righteous individuals and wicked sinners all went to *Sheol* on their demise (Ezekiel 32:18–32). No reward or punishment existed for earthly deeds, words, or thoughts.

The Eternal ultimately became the God of the entire universe for the ancient Jews. Thus, by the time of the Babylonian exile in the sixth century B.C.E., the Divine power came to be viewed as extending over *Sheol*. God took control over the Netherworld and, thus, God's power could save humans from the grasp of *Sheol*. As the Psalmist writes, "But God will redeem my life from the clutches of *Sheol*, for the Divine will take me." (Psalms 49:16). *Sheol* became a place for punishing the wicked.

In light of the ethical stance of the Jewish sages, each individual came to be seen as rewarded or punished in proportion to his or her righteousness or transgressions during life. Good people were viewed as living a blessed existence on earth or in the world of souls; while the wicked were condemned by God to *Sheol*, the subterranean realm, as a punishment. As the *Book of Proverbs* states, "For a [righteous] person, the path of life leads upward, in order to avoid *Sheol* below" (Proverbs 15:24).

PURGATORY IN THE RABBINIC TEACHINGS

The rabbis' afterlife teachings rest on the notion of Purgatory as a realm of postdeath punishment for those who did not live a righteous life—a life filled with good deeds, words and thoughts, including love, compassion, and forgiveness. Actions that brought about punishments in Purgatory included adultery, pride (or a lack of humility), anger, and an excessive preoccupation with materialistic indulgence.[2] For the rabbis, Purgatory represented Divine justice in action. In Purgatory, each individual faced the consequences of his or her thoughts, words, and deeds during life.

The descriptions of Purgatory evolved over numerous centuries. Initially, the rabbis spoke of the various original names for Purgatory, each based on a biblical passage: for instance, *Sheol*, as discussed earlier; Destruction (Isaiah 38:17); Horrible Pit (Isaiah 14:15; Ezekiel 26:20, 28:8; Psalms 40:3, 55:24); and the traditional Netherworld of Torment. These various names came to represent realms in Purgatory, a place beneath the earth, to which the wicked were sent for punishment according to their worldly actions, words, and thoughts.

---

[2]Raphael, *Afterlife*, pp. 142–144, 303.

SEVEN REALMS OF PURGATORY

As the concept of Purgatory evolved, the different strands of Jewish tradition delineated its topography and described the various types of suffering souls encountered there. The frightening portrayals sought to convince Jews of the ghastly consequences of their earthly wickedness.

For over one thousand years Jewish sages have portrayed Purgatory as consisting of seven realms or tiers, each offering a punishment of a different tormenting nature. Particular categories of sinners are consigned to one (or more) of the seven regions of Purgatory to receive specific types of purifications based on their respective sins.

According to the mystical tradition:

> [Purgatory] has seven doors which open into seven habitations; and there are also seven types of sinners: evildoers, worthless ones, sinners, the wicked, corrupters, mockers, and the arrogant ones; and corresponding with them are the habitations in [Purgatory], for each kind a particular place, all according to grade (Zohar IV, 150b).

The various levels of Purgatory were portrayed as having avenging angels and designated leaders. According to one writer of the medieval interpretative materials, the designated leaders for six compartments of Purgatory (the first compartment, *Sheol*, was viewed as lacking a leader) are as follows:

1. Absalom—tenth century B.C.E., son of King David, who killed his brother Amnon, who had raped his sister Tamar. He led an unsuccessful rebellion against David in which his army was defeated and he was killed (II Samuel 13–19)

2. Korah—who, together with Dathan and Abiram and 250 Israelite leaders, rebelled against Moses and Aaron (Num-

bers 16); as punishment the earth opened and swallowed them (Numbers 26:10)

3. Jeroboam II—eighth century B.C.E., King of Israel whose rule was marred by corruption, which was denounced by the prophets Amos and Hosea (I Kings 14)

4. Ahab—King of Israel in ninth century B.C.E., who was reproached by the prophet Elijah for seizing Naboth's vineyard (I Kings 21)

5. Micah—Jewish prophet in the eighth century B.C.E., who lived in Judah and defended the people against oppression by the ruling classes; he prophesied the destruction of Judah and exile to Babylon

6. Elisha ben Avuyah—lived in the second century C.E. and came to doubt the unity of God, Divine providence, and reward and punishment, ultimately renouncing Judaism.[3]

In rather graphic detail, the medieval interpretative literature depicts the geography of Purgatory spelling out the fate of the wicked:

1. There are five kinds of punishments in [Purgatory], and Isaiah, the son of Amos, saw them all. He entered the first compartment and saw there two men carrying pails of water on their shoulders, and they pour that water into a pit, which, however, never fills. Isaiah said to God, "O You who [unveils] all that is hidden, unveil to me the secret of this." And the Spirit of God answered, "These are the men who coveted the property of their neighbors, and this is their punishment."

---

[3]Adapted from "This is the Description of Gehinnom (Hell)" in *The Chronicles of Jerahmeel*, XXI:6, trans. M. Gaster (New York: Ktav, 1971), pp. 45–46. The inclusion of the prophet Micah in this list of leaders is difficult to fathom.

2. He entered the second compartment, and he saw two men hanging by their tongues, and he said, "O You who [unveils] the hidden, reveal to me the secret of this." God answered, "These are the men who slandered, therefore they are thus punished."

3. He entered the third compartment, and he saw there men hanging by their organs. He said, "O You who [unveils] the hidden, reveal to me the secret of this." And God answered, "These are the men who neglected their own wives and committed adultery with the daughters of Israel."

4. He entered the fourth compartment and saw there women hanging by their breasts, and he said, "O You who [unveils] the hidden, reveal to me the secret of this." And God answered, "These are the women who uncovered their hair . . . and stay in the open marketplace to [breast feed] their children in order to attract the gaze of men and to make them sin; therefore, they are punished thus."

5. He entered the fifth compartment and found it full of smoke. There were all the princes, chiefs, and great men, and Pharaoh, the wicked, presides over them and watches at the gate of [Purgatory], and he [says] unto them, "Why did you not learn from me when I was in Egypt?" Thus he sits there and watches at the gates of [Purgatory].

6. There are seven compartments in [Purgatory], and in each of them are 7,000 rooms, in each room 7,000 windows, in each window (recess) there are 7,000 vessels filled with venom, all destined for slanderous writers and iniquitous judges.[4]

---

[4]Adapted from "This is the Description of Gehinnom (Hell)" in *The Chronicles of Jerahmeel*, XVI, pp. 36–37.

As a disembodied soul journeys through one or more levels of Purgatory, it encounters various mythical beings, including Dumah (previously described on pages 104–105 of Chapter 5 as the angel serving as the soul's guardian–caretaker in the immediate postdeath period), who also functions as the guardian of Purgatory, patrolling its entrance. According to Jewish sources, Dumah, working with a myriad of helpers, delivers the newly arrived souls to the various gatekeepers of Purgatory's seven regions. These gatekeepers then close "the gates of flaming fire" (Zohar II, 237b).

Subordinate to Dumah, the mystics suggest that there are three specific chiefs of Purgatory, namely, Destruction, Anger, and Wrath, who regulate the punishment of sinners guilty of murder, incest, and idolatry. Souls also come upon special angels who are appointed for each realm of Purgatory to carry out specific punishments according to the sins of the wicked.

METAPHORIC ELEMENTS OF PURGATORY

In addition to the seven realms so vividly portrayed in the medieval literature, the Jewish sages speak of the metaphoric elements of Purgatory. Seeing a blazing fire of abnormal intensity as well as snow and ice, they gave free rein to their imagination. The rabbis also viewed Purgatory as a place of darkness.

Commentators subsequently built on the fire and ice motif. One medieval writer notes, "*Sheol* consists half of fire and half of [ice], and when the sinners contained therein emerge from the fire they are tortured by the [ice], and when they emerge from the [ice] the fire burns them. . . . "[5]

---

[5]*Ibid., The Chronicles of Jerahmeel*, XVII: 2, p. 38.

This same medieval author explains the fire element in more detail as follows:

Five different kinds of fires are in [Purgatory]: one devours and absorbs, another absorbs and does not devour, [another devours but does not absorb], while another, again, neither devours nor absorbs. There is further fire devouring fire. There are coals big as mountains, and coals big as hills, and coals huge like unto the Dead Sea, and coals like huge stones. There are rivers of pitch and sulphur flowing and fuming and seething.[6]

The Jewish mystics describe the process of purification by fire for souls polluted by earthly filth. The fire, which burns twenty-four hours each day (except on the Sabbath), corresponds to a human's hot, sinful passions. The more defiled an individual, the more he or she experienced unbridled lust on earth, particularly sexuality, the stronger the need for the fire of purification that burns out the sins of passion. Thus, a fire of abnormal intensity burns in Purgatory in order to consume each individual's accumulated contamination during his or her life.

The mystical literature suggests that the mode of punishment in Purgatory consists of a combination of fire as well as snow and ice. The fire and snow punishment is described as follows:

Rabbi Hizkiah . . . said that sinners are punished in [Purgatory] twelve months, half with fire, half with snow. When they go into the fire, they say: "This is really [Purgatory]!" When they go into the snow, they say: "This is the real winter of the Almighty." They begin by exclaiming "Alas!" and then exclaim "Woe." The supreme punishment is with snow (Zohar II, 238b).

---

[6]*Ibid., The Chronicles of Jerahmeel,* XIV: 4–5, p. 33.

For the Jewish mystics, ice represents the quality of mercy extended to sinners to cool the fiery flames of passion or anger. Snow is also seen as freezing out the sins of calculation, the failings of an unloving, unforgiving heart.

TIME SPENT IN PURGATORY

Jewish sources generally view the period of time a soul spends in Purgatory as finite.[7] In other words, damnation is not eternal. The soul's journey through Purgatory, and the accompanying purification from earthly life's defilements, eventually ends.

Jewish sages throughout the ages reiterated that the soul typically completes its period of purgation and purification in Purgatory after a maximum of twelve months. According to tradition, one year represents the length of time needed to extract most of the soul's impurities and prepare it for its ongoing postmortem journey. Because time does not exist in the World to Come, however, who knows what one year feels like in Purgatory.

Despite this general conclusion, various strands of the Jewish tradition—rabbinical, medieval, and mystical—asserted that certain classes of sinners were eternally condemned to the various realms of Purgatory. For example, one medieval commentator noted:

Three descend to [Purgatory] forever, and do not ascend anymore—the man who commits adultery, who blames his [neighbor] in public, and who is guilty of perjury. Others say, Those who seek [honor] for themselves by slandering their [neighbors], and those who make intrigues between man and woman in order to create strife among them.[8]

---

[7]Raphael, *Afterlife*, pp. 144–145, 303–305.
[8]"This is the Description of Gehinnom (Hell)" in *The Chronicles of Jerahmeel*, XV: 6, p. 35.

These teachings of eternal damnation served an ethical, educational purpose. By demonstrating the terrible consequences of earthly life, these notions were designed to motivate people to lives of good words and deeds or, at least, to sincere repentance. Those who never repented might be condemned to eternal punishment. According to the mystical tradition:

> Rabbi Jose said, "Woe to the wicked who will not repent of their sins before the Almighty while they are still in this world. For when a man repents of his sins and feels remorse for them, the Holy [Blessed] One ... forgives them. But those who cling to their sins and refuse to repent of them will in the end descend to [Purgatory] and never come up again" (Zohar I, 66a).

However, the teachings of an eternal punishment for souls in Purgatory remained a minority view among Jewish sages. According to the mainstream of the Jewish tradition, the vast proportion of souls, after a transitory experience in Purgatory, are sufficiently purified to enter the realm of Paradise. It is important to note that only a relatively few individuals, such as Chaim, the focal point of Reb Elimelech's story in Chapter 1, skip Purgatory and go directly to Paradise. Those who are more, but not totally, "righteous" experience a shorter and easier purification process in Purgatory.

TRADITIONAL JEWISH RITUALS

As discussed in Chapter 6, after the death of a parent, the traditional mourning period lasts for twelve months (or thirty days for other close relatives) from the day of death. Children recite a special memorial prayer, the Mourner's Kaddish,[9] for a deceased par-

---

[9]For background on the Mourner's Kaddish I have drawn on Tzvi Rabinowicz (1989), *A Guide to Life: Jewish Laws and Customs of Mourning* (Northvale, NJ: Jason Aronson),

ent. Although originally recited for a parent only by sons (but now by both sons and daughters, at least in nonOrthodox congregations), it has become customary for survivors to recite the Mourner's Kaddish for a child, a spouse, sibling, or other close relatives, such as a grandparent.

The origins of the Mourner's Kaddish are quite mysterious. Although prayers for the dead are mentioned in the *Books of Maccabbes* and echoes of the Kaddish reach us from early rabbinic writings, the Mourner's Kaddish in its present form dates from the period of the Gaonism, in the seventh century C.E., some 1,400 years ago. By the thirteenth century C.E. it became the practice for mourners to recite the Kaddish as a link in the chain of being, situating the living in the procession of generations.

The period for saying the Mourner's Kaddish (eleven months from the day of death for parents) corresponds roughly to the twelve months that Jewish sages proclaim a soul spends in Purgatory. Mourners recite the Kaddish for only eleven months to avoid any implication that the soul of a parent requires the full term in Purgatory.

A mourner traditionally recites the Kaddish prayer publicly at daily (morning and evening) religious services. A minyan—the requisite number of ten Jewish adults, traditionally adult males, but in an egalitarian era, men and women in nonOrthodox congregations—must be present.

Public recitation of the Kaddish offers the possibility of communal support and the embrace of others as well as creating a sense of community to help overcome the isolation and loneliness often

---

Footnote 9 (*continued*)

pp. 69–79; Maurice Lamm (1969), *The Jewish Way in Death and Mourning* (New York: Jonathan David), pp. 149–175; Central Conference of American Rabbis (1988), *Rabbi's Manual* (New York: Central Conference of American Rabbis), pp. 254–255; *Jewish Insights on Death and Mourning*, ed. Jack Riemer (New York: Schocken, 1995), pp. 168–182; and Gershom, *Beyond the Ashes*, pp. 69, 203–204.

encountered in bereavement. The saying of Kaddish also unites a group of mourners, who regularly attend worship services, in a time of seeming helplessness and despair.

The Mourner's Kaddish represents a prayer of praise for and glorification of God as well as a supplication for the Eternal's rule and a plea for peace for all humanity. It does not refer to the dead, mourning, or the afterlife. Rather it is concerned with life in this world and the day when the earth will reflect godliness. It offers a message of comfort, hope, and peace. The bereaved gradually regain their perspective as they once again see sunny blue skies, glorious flowers, and beautiful birds.

A well-known story in the Talmud helps supply a key, enabling us to unlock the secrets of the Kaddish. Rabbi Meir, we're told, lost both of his sons on the same day. It was on a Sabbath afternoon when he was teaching in the House of Study. His wife, Beruriah, did not give him the news on his return so as not to sadden his Sabbath-joy. She waited until the evening. After he had eaten, she asked her husband: "I have a question. Some time ago, a friend came and gave me some jewels for safekeeping. Today, that person demands them back. What should I do?" Rabbi Meir unhesitatingly responded, "You must return the jewels." Then she led her husband to the room where their children lay dead. She said, "These are the jewels I must return." Sobbing, Rabbi Meir repeated the words of Job: "God gave and the Eternal has taken back. Blessed be the name of the Holy One" (Job 1:21).[10]

In the Kaddish prayer, the mourner publicly declares his or her great faith in God's exalted greatness and goodness as well as his or her submission to God's eternal will and justness as follows:

Let the glory of God be extolled, let the Eternal's great name be magnified and sanctified in the world created according to the Divine

[10]Adapted from Dr. Joseph H. Hertz, *The Authorised Daily Prayer Book*, rev. ed. (New York: Bloch, 1985), p. 270.

will. May God's spiritual foundation soon prevail in our own day, in our own lives, and the life of all of Israel, and let us say: Amen.

Let God's great name be blessed now and for ever and ever.

Let the name and the presence of the Blessed Holy One be praised, glorified, exalted, extolled, and honored, though the Almighty is beyond all praises, songs, and expressions that we can utter, and let us say: Amen.

For us and for everyone, may the abundance of peace and the promise of life's goodness come true and let us say: Amen.

May the God, who causes peace to reign in the high heavens, bring peace to us, to all Israel, and to everyone and let us say: Amen.[11]

Saying the Kaddish prayer represents an act of reverence for a deceased parent or other close relative. As such, it's a way of remembering the dead with respect. It serves to give meaning and value to the life of the departed and to strengthen family bonds. It also helps the mourner hold onto his or her memories and perceive with greater clarity the deceased's legacy.

Daily recitation of the Kaddish provides emotional and psychological healing. Saying Kaddish helps a child or other family member gradually accept the death and adjust to the loss of a parent or other close relative. It also helps a mourner stay in contact with the

---

[11]Adapted from *Ibid.*, p. 213; and Central Conference of American Rabbis (1975), *Gates of Prayer: The New Union Prayerbook* (New York: Central Conference of American Rabbis), pp. 629–630. Eight other ways to say Kaddish are set forth in Anita Diamant (1998), *Saying Kaddish: How to Comfort the Dying, Bury the Dead, and Mourn as a Jew* (New York: Schocken), pp. 203–212.

ongoing "griefwork" process, which includes awareness of the immensity of the loss, adjusting to an earthly environment where the deceased is missing, and forming new relationships.

It allows for a catharsis of emotions. Saying the Kaddish prayer helps a mourner pay more careful attention to the various feelings and emotions that typically arise as a result of the loss of a beloved family member.

Rabbi Zalman Schachter-Shalomi, founder of the Jewish Renewal Movement, uses the phrase, "Going to Kaddish College" in describing the function of the Kaddish process. The mourner learns a lot about him or herself, the decedent, and his or her relationship with the departed; perhaps more, in some general sense, than he or she learned in college.

Schachter-Shalomi tells the following story about his father's death:

> . . . I was driving home in my truck "Beryl." Soon after I started out, a driver on the road cut me off. I instantly let out a string of curses— Polish, Yiddish . . . every obscenity in my vocabulary.
>
> Then I stopped myself as I heard the echoing of my father's voice. It was exactly as he would curse and swear while driving at the wheel. I said aloud: "Papa, this is one of yours! This one you can have back."
>
> I realized that I was just beginning to sort out . . . my inheritance from Papa, to understand what he had given me that I could affirm as my own, and what was his, not mine.[12]

Through the Kaddish process, which represents the sorting out of one's inheritance on a number of levels—intellectual, emotional, and spiritual—the mourner achieves a sense of inner peace and completion with the departed. Gradually, the survivor goes from

---

[12]Simcha Steven Paull (1986), *Judaism's Contribution to the Psychology of Death and Dying* (Ph.D. diss. California Institute of Integral Studies), p. 367.

denial to the acknowledgment and acceptance of the reality of death and his or her loss. Experiencing a feeling of renewal, the mourner moves forward to a life less defined by attachment to the deceased.

In addition to reciting the Kaddish prayer, according to Jewish tradition, a mourner makes charitable contributions in the deceased's name. He or she also dedicates other acts of kindness to the decedent's memory.

RECITING THE MOURNER'S KADDISH TO FACILITATE THE SOUL'S AFTERLIFE JOURNEY

Perceiving that the living and the departed are interconnected, the Kaddish process performs a soul-guiding function,[13] enabling the bereaved and soul of the deceased to engage in an interactive dialogue. The living can communicate with the departed on two levels. First, saying Kaddish helps mediate the continuing relationship between the survivors and the soul of a dead loved one. Second, recital of the Mourner's Prayer by the living may help redeem a soul on its purification journey in Purgatory. In other words, saying Kaddish affects the postmortem destiny of the soul of the departed in Purgatory.

The recitation of the Kaddish facilitates the completion of the relationship between the living and the soul in Purgatory during the postdeath period. In some family situations, the bereaved and the soul of the deceased continue to work out their previous, stormy relationship. The survivors use the mourning process—specifically, the recital of the Kaddish prayer—to finish their old emotional business and deal with a variety of the negative emotions and resentments.

---

[13]*Ibid.*, pp. 368–370; and Raphael, *Afterlife*, pp. 387–388.

For these families, Purgatory may be viewed as the process of purging the emotional "stuff" swept under the rug between (and among) family members during the life just lived. The Kaddish process represents a time for healing relationships, particularly negative feelings and lingering resentments not mended during the deceased's lifetime, including issues that weren't worked out and difficulties never really confronted.

One hasidic tale concerns Reb Abraham Hamalach—known as the Angel, the son of the Maggid of Mezhirich, who lived from 1740 to 1776—and his widow. It goes as follows:

> One night his widow had a dream. She saw a vast hall and in it thrones, set in a semicircle. On each throne sat one of the great. A door opened. One who looked like the others, entered. It was Abraham, her late husband. He said: "Friends, my wife bears a grudge against me because in my earthly life I lived apart from her. She is right, and therefore I must obtain her forgiveness." His widow cried out: "With all my heart I forgive you," and awoke comforted.[14]

This story indicates that the Jewish mystics perceived that consciousness survives bodily demise. Previously incomplete relationships require healing for both the surviving bereaved and the disembodied soul.

Even ten or fifteen minutes of brief but open communication, in a dream or through a meditation or visualization, can close the gap created by decades of separation. Resolving old emotions and relationships reminds me of the story of two people who have been pulling feverishly on opposite ends of a rope. When one lets go of his or her end, all of the tension between them dissipates.

But often it takes more than fifteen minutes. Going through the

---

[14]Adapted from Martin Buber (1975), *Tales of the Hasidim: The Early Masters*, trans. Olga Marx (New York: Schocken), p. 117.

rather lengthy Kaddish process helps some mourners resolve their churning, incomplete emotions about a departed family member. The mourner may pour out his or her strong but previously unexpressed feelings, ask for answers to serious questions, and tell the soul of the deceased stories that have been kept secret or perhaps reflect negatively on the departed. Asking for forgiveness, a keynote to Spiritual Judaism, the survivor may be more open to listening to the soul's response, which may take the form of an apology to the living. By getting things off their chests, reciting the Mourner's Prayer gradually helps the survivors reclaim their lives, freeing them to go on, to live unburdened by whatever was previously unresolved with the deceased.

It's often an interactive process between the living and the dead as pleasant thoughts replace painful memories. Let's imagine the following Kaddish dialogue between a son and the soul of his deceased father.

Initially:

Son: I'm really angry at you.

Father: You're rotten.

Ten months later:

Son: You were never around for me when I was growing up.

Father: You don't know what my life was like.

Son: I miss you, Dad. Tell me your story. I feel so sad.

Father: With what I had, I tried the best I could.

Son: I never had a chance to say "I love you" before you died.

Father: I'm sorry that I wasn't the best of fathers. I want to bless you.

Son: I love you. I realize now what you gave me was good.

Father: I bless you. Now, go on and live your own life.[15]

Through the Kaddish dialogue, the son can pour out his memories; things he wished he could have told his father during life; his scars from the lack of a strong, fatherly presence; something he always wanted to hear his father say; something his father didn't understand; or something he resented about his father.

Gradually, parent and child achieve a new opening as the gulf that separated them over the years dissolves into love, forgiveness, and reconciliation. Through an exploration of issues, even after death, a relationship can evolve, initially imperceptible yet ultimately, quite remarkable. Kaddish process keeps the dialogue going until the living generally say all that they need to tell the soul of the departed.

On a different level, the Kaddish process may also affect the destiny of the soul of the deceased in the postmortem realms. The mystical tradition suggests that saying Kaddish assists a parent's (or close relative's) soul during its purification in Purgatory. By attaining a sense of inner peace and resolving relationship and emotional issues pertaining to a loved one and his or her demise, the mourner beneficially impacts the soul during its period of cleansing. As the living recite the Mourner's Prayer and enter into a dialogue with the soul, a Kaddish rap, to put it in contemporary terms, the soul, as a disembodied state of consciousness, may gradually perceive and feel the consequences of its negative conduct, words, and thoughts during life. Forgiving a parent (or other close relative) for any hurt or harm, the mystics maintain, helps the parent's (or other close

---

[15]Adapted from a lecture by Simcha Paull Raphael, "Jewish Views of the Afterlife," May 21, 1997.

relative's) soul resolve feelings of guilt and shame. This process assists in cleansing the slate. The soul's incomplete emotions are gradually purified. Thus, saying Kaddish may provide a source of inspiration and guidance for a soul of the departed, thereby diminishing its suffering in Purgatory.

Although problematic for individuals without children, the following folk legend illustrates the significance of the Mourner's Kaddish for the soul as well as the connection between the living and the deceased:

> Rabbi Akiva [the great first century C.E. rabbi, warrior and martyr] once saw the shadowy figure of a man carrying a load of wood on his shoulders and groaning under his load. "What ails you?" asked the Rabbi. "I am one of those forlorn souls condemned for his sins to the agony of hell-fire. I must procure the wood and myself prepare my place of torment." "And is there no hope for you?" inquired the rabbi in great compassion. "Yes, if my little son, whom I left behind an infant, is taught to utter the Kaddish and cause the assembly of worshipers to respond "Amen, may God's great name be praised for ever and ever.'" Rabbi Akiva resolved to search for the family and the deceased's infant son. He found that the mother had remarried, this time to a nonJew; and he found that the child had not been circumcised (i.e., ritually initiated into the covenant of Abraham). Rabbi Akiva took the child under his care and taught him to lisp the Kaddish. Soon, a heavenly message assured him that through the son's prayer, the father had been released from Purgatory.[16]

Also, by performing good deeds, including making charitable contributions in the decedent's memory, the living can strengthen their relationship with the soul of the departed. The merit these beneficent, life affirming activities generate are said to represent one

---

[16]Adapted from Hertz, *The Authorised Daily Prayer Book*, p. 271.

or more additional assets attached to the soul on its postmortem journey.

SUGGESTIONS FOR SPIRITUAL SEEKERS AND OTHERS WRESTLING WITH GRIEF

From the viewpoint of Spiritual Judaism, observance of the Kaddish ritual and the recital of the Mourner's Prayer is far less important than the soul-guiding concepts underpinning the process. In other words, it's the process more than the rote recital of a prayer. Surviving loved ones may find attendance at daily worship services, to put it bluntly, rather dull, lacking in spiritual immediacy and intimacy, to say nothing of being inconvenient. Arising in the dark and cold of winter and going every evening isn't easy.

Bereaved spiritual seekers and others wrestling with grief who want to escape tradition and devise something personal often find it helpful to set aside time on a regular basis each day for a number of weeks or months (and in some cases, even a year or more) to grieve freely, sort out their feelings, and continue to forge a link between the world of the survivors and the realm of the dead. Studies indicate that as many as sixty-six percent of widows see or feel a deceased husband's presence shortly after his death. As many as seventy-five percent of all bereaved parents have contact with their child's soul within one year of his or her death.[17]

Through spontaneous, unstructured, individual prayers from the heart, silent meditations, and visualizations, strive to stay in contact with the soul of the departed and experience the continued sense of their ongoing relationship. Consider getting and making notes in a journal, taking long walks even in an urban environment, or look-

---

[17]Raymond Moody, M.D. (1993), with Paul Perry, *Reunions: Visionary Encounters with Departed Loved Ones* (New York: Villard), p. x.

ing at old photo albums, a piece of jewelry, or some other special object. Although tears come with remembrance, it's whatever works as a focal point for a personalized means of coming to terms with and healing the grief.

Some of us can't believe we'll never see the departed again. We're lonely. We miss them so genuinely. We want to talk with them. The raw feelings of loss continue to pervade our life.

Initially, struggling back and forth, we're unable to separate. We're tied by an intense bond of love. Gradually, the living learn to let go. We accept our own finiteness and impermanence and that of the departed. We adjust to a changed environment and begin to form new relationships.

Recognizing that, according to Jewish tradition, consciousness survives bodily death, continue to say your goodbyes, express your respect and gratitude, and send loving, freeing thoughts to the soul of the deceased, not thoughts that would encourage its attachment to the material world.

As difficult as it is with a beloved family member or friend, do not brood excessively over the departed. Of course, express your respect, honor, and love for the departed. As the Jewish tradition teaches, God did not create us to destroy us. Each soul is destined for further development and a better existence.

Several months after my mother's death, I saw her in a dream. I couldn't tell what clothes she was wearing, but she looked in her mid-seventies, about the same age as when she died. She seemed so healthy and radiant. She was wholly joyful and at peace. Smiling happily, she indicated, "I'm fine." From what I saw and heard, she was no longer in pain, as she had been the last two weeks of her life. I came to realize that death does not end life. Life continues, albeit on a different plane.

Expressing positive sentiments, particularly praying for cleansing and healing, enables, the Jewish sages teach, the soul to complete its purification process in Purgatory more quickly and more thoroughly. By opening your heart to the Eternal, invoke God's love and compassion for the soul of the departed. Thus, the living can assist and elevate a soul on its journey in the postmortem realms.

In some more troubled family situations, the postdeath spiritual process may facilitate the reconciliation and completion of a difficult relationship between the living and the soul of the departed. These family members need to focus on the unresolved emotional issues, painful memories, regrets, and any lingering feelings that came with death.

As we've seen in Chapter 2, forgiveness plays a large role in Spiritual Judaism. The living can help the soul of the deceased by: reviewing their relationship; asking for forgiveness by the soul for any past transgressions on their part; expressing their willingness to forgive the departed for his or her prior deeds, words, or thoughts; and encouraging self-forgiveness.

Strive to openly and honestly express your continuing gratitude as well as your lingering resentments and tensions with the departed. Try to see from the decedent's perspective anything they now perceive as a "negative" in your relationship, including regrets, fears, anger, guilt, sorrow, loneliness, or anxieties.

In pouring out and releasing their feelings, striving to make amends, and unburdening their guilt, diligently listen for the departed's response, which may consist of an expression of forgiveness. As is true of many situations, both sides may need to acknowledge their joint responsibility in order to overcome the anger, the fears, and the guilt emanating from mistakes in their relationship.

You may find the following unguided meditation (or visualization) useful in opening the channel of communication between yourself and the soul of the departed, in achieving a sense of completion with respect to previously unresolved issues, and in quieting your mind and nourishing your inner essence. Speaking from your inner heart, try to enter into a dialogue with the soul of the deceased for ten to fifteen minutes, making an effort to express what lies at the root of your continued separation. Continuing an ongoing, daily, interactive dialogue focused on forgiveness and letting go of the past will hopefully open lines of communication, permitting alienation to fall away.

Forgiveness and Lovingkindness Meditation (or Visualization)

Introductory Instructions. Create a warm, welcoming atmosphere, an environment of serenity and spaciousness for the journey. Lower the lights in your room.

Close your eyes, sit quietly, calm and relax your body. Breathe in and out normally, feeling where your breath flows into and out of your body. Adjust your breathing so that the in and out breaths are of the same length.

Feel yourself surrounded by warmth and love. Allow any anger to dissolve into the warmth and love.

With each breath, breathe in warmth. Feel the warmth nourishing you. Breathe in love and feel the openness that love creates in you. Allow the warmth and love to give rise to forgiveness. The power of forgiveness is great.

Visualize the deceased. With a new state of openness, invite him/her into your heart. Notice whatever blocks his/her approach to your heart: the problem, the hurt, the fear, the anger, the guilt, or whatever. Enter into and continue a dialogue with the departed until there's nothing more to say. Now, try to let the deceased through to your heart. Let go of the pride that holds onto resentment. Allow the pain of old hurts to dissolve.

In your heart, say "I forgive you for whatever you did in the past, whether intentionally or unintentionally, through your deeds, words, or thoughts, that caused me pain or hurt." Repeat the words: "I forgive you." Allowing the forgiveness to grow, let go of your resentments, your anger, and your hurt, and open unconditionally to love and compassion.

Again, visualize the deceased. Does he/she resent you? Did you cause him/her pain? Did the departed put you out of his/her heart? With a new state of openness invite the deceased into your heart. Notice whatever blocks his/her approach to your heart. Try to let the deceased through to your heart.

From the bottom of your heart ask for forgiveness. Say "I ask for your forgiveness for what I did in the past, whether intentionally or unintentionally, through my deeds, words, or thoughts, that caused you pain or hurt." Repeat the words: "Please forgive me." Again, let yourself be touched by the possibility of forgiveness. Ask him/ her to let go of his/her anger and hurt and let you back into his/her heart. Feel his or her forgiveness.

Let your heart fill with forgiveness and lovingkindness for yourself. May I be happy and at peace, free from anger, pain, fear, guilt, sorrow, and doubt. May I be filled with love.

Concluding Instructions. Come back to the here and now. Take time to ease yourself back. Slowly bring your awareness back to your body. Feel yourself back in the room and open your eyes.

To sort out your relationship with the deceased, you may find it useful, as have many others, to put in a journal, on paper, or in a letter to the departed, the specific unresolved issues, the exact difficulties never adequately confronted, the previously unspoken words, uncommunicated thoughts and feelings, the anger, pain, guilt, sadness, and anything you yearn for. This detailed, focused, written expression of a troubled relationship may better enable you to enter into a dialogue with the deceased and see things from his or her viewpoint. Also, write down several of the departed's redeeming, positive qualities. Your feelings toward the decedent may gradually shift, enabling you to work out your unfinished relationship, incomplete emotions, and turbulent feelings and get on with the business of living your life. You will be able to finally say your genuine and lasting goodbyes.

We each grieve in our own way and in our own time frame. Gradually, the living, although maintaining their love and respect for the deceased, accept the reality of death and let go of their identity with and attachment to the departed. Grief, sadness, and guilt lessen. They realize that the relationship—good or bad (and for most of us, it's a mix of good and bad)—is over. A sense of loss remains, but somehow its much softer and more gentle. As Leon Wieseltier puts it in his personal and impassioned record of his quest for the meaning of the kaddish, "Slowly you acquire a standpoint from which to offer resistance to your sorrow, until your sorrow becomes just another of your parts. It is not erased, it is conquered; and it is conquered when it is contextualized. Context is another name for consolation."[18]Free to go on with life, they find new interests and friendships to replace what has been lost.

Remaining in contact with the soul of the departed often helps the living. The following anecdote illustrates this point.

After many years of dating, living single, being in and out of relationships, Betsy, a young woman in her early 30's, met the man she would marry. While there was much delight in this experience of love and in the anticipation of marriage, Betsy's joy was infused with deep sadness as her mother's health continued to deteriorate. For Betsy, life and death, joy and sadness were deeply intertwined. Two days before her actual wedding, a mock ceremony was performed at her mother's hospital bedside, so Betsy might share this precious event with her mother in the only way possible. The day

---

[18]Leon Wiesteltier (1998), *Kaddish* (New York: Knopf), p. 548.

after Betsy and her beloved were actually married, they left for a long-awaited honeymoon.

The sun, sand, and sea of the Caribbean were soothing to the newlyweds, giving them an intimate time to bond and begin married life. But on the third day, in the middle of the night, Betsy sensed her mother's presence at her bedside saying goodbye. Only hours later, at the crack of dawn, Betsy received a telephone call informing her that she had to return home for her mother's funeral.

For many months Betsy went through an intense grief experience. You might imagine how difficult it was, trying to begin married life while dealing with the loss of the mother whom she loved so deeply. And yet, above all, it was the memory of her mother's presence in the room that night that gave Betsy strength to cope with her loss and to affirm her new life in the face of death.

Then, one year after her mom's death, in a dream, Betsy saw her mother in a luminescent blue dress. Waving to her, Betsy's mother told her, "Everything is OK. I love you. Go ahead with your life." The dream was a great comfort to Betsy. She now felt completely free to create a new and meaningful life with her husband.[19]

According to the Jewish tradition, the soul of the departed only spends a finite period of time undergoing purification in Purgatory. With the completion of its work in Purgatory, the Jewish sages proclaim that the soul continues on to its destiny. In next stage, to which we now turn, the soul enters the realm of Lower Paradise. Then, the soul goes to Upper Paradise. Through its journey in Paradise, the soul discovers a world of emotional, intellectual, and spiritual bliss. The soul freely experiences the loftiest feelings of joy and ecstasy, without any limitation.

---

[19]Adapted from a lecture by Simcha Paull Raphael, "Jewish Views of the Afterlife," May 21, 1997.

CHAPTER EIGHT

PARADISE: THE SOUL'S HEAVENLY VISIONS

C ontinuing our journey through the world of souls, this chapter examines the notion of Paradise in the Jewish tradition, focusing on the two stages of Paradise: Lower Paradise and Upper Paradise.[1] Again, we should not view these two levels of Paradise—the Garden of Eden or *Gan Eden* in Hebrew—as an actual abode of the righteous after death. Rather, Paradise represents a state of consciousness.

In the postmortem realm of Paradise, the soul continues its evolutionary journey of emotional, intellectual, and spiritual growth.

---

[1] I have drawn on the notion of Paradise as presented in Simcha Paull Raphael (1994), *Jewish Views of the Afterlife* (Northvale, NJ: Jason Aronson), pp. 149–154, 184–206, 296–298, 308–313, 348–351, 388–391. Various concepts of Paradise are also developed in Anne Brener (1993), *Mourning & Mitzvah: A Guided Journal for Walking the Mourner's Path Through Grief to Healing* (Woodstock, VT: Jewish Lights Publishing), pp. 199–200; Yonassan Gershom (1992), *Beyond the Ashes: Cases of Reincarnation from the Holocaust* (Virginia Beach, VA: A.R.E. Press), p. 68; and Rifat Sonsino and Daniel B. Syme (1990), *What Happens After I Die? Jewish Views of Life After Death* (New York: UAHC Press,), pp. 28–29.

Paradise represents neither a static experience nor a soul's final destination. It's rest and recreation for the soul. On its postdeath journey, the soul ultimately advances to even higher, more transcendent spiritual levels.

We'll also explore two Jewish rituals, *Yahrzeit* and *Yizkor*, designed to teach us to remember the departed and help elevate a soul to the loftier reaches of Paradise. Suggestions are provided for spiritual seekers who wish to establish (or maintain) a genuine bond of connection with the soul of a departed.

THE SOUL'S JOURNEY IN LOWER PARADISE: AN OVERVIEW

Lower Paradise serves as a transit stage between Purgatory and Upper Paradise. In the Lower Paradise, each soul continues the purification process begun in Purgatory and prepares for entry into Upper Paradise.

Souls of nearly all the departed who do not immediately merit admission into Upper Paradise are assigned to a lower realm, namely, Lower Paradise, according to the merits accumulated in their respective immediate past earthly lifetimes. In Lower Paradise, each soul experiences the emotional, intellectual, and spiritual bliss appropriate to its past attainments.

According to Jewish sources, Paradise—whether Lower Paradise or Upper Paradise—represents a heavenly realm where souls, as disembodied states of consciousness, reside for an unspecified but not eternal timeframe. The period a soul spends in Lower Paradise can, perhaps, best be viewed as representing the interval needed for further refining, completing, and working out an individual's personality on an emotional plane as well as for further developing the soul's intellectual and spiritual levels.

The last vestiges of the decedent's earthly personality and his or her most recent personal life experiences slowly ebb in Lower Paradise.[2] Incomplete desires, attachments, and emotions are experienced there. What is personal and impermanent gradually dissipates. In Lower Paradise, the soul experiences an increasing degree of emotional pleasure.

ENTRY INTO LOWER PARADISE

After completing its cleansing in Purgatory, the mystical literature describes the soul's preparation for entry to Lower Paradise as follows:

> At first, the soul is taken to a spot . . . in the interior of [Purgatory] where souls are cleansed and purified before they enter Lower Paradise. Two angel messengers stand at the gate of Paradise and call aloud to the chieftains who have charge of that spot in [Purgatory], summoning them to receive that soul, and during the whole process of purification, they continue to utter aloud repeatedly the word *Hinnom* ["here they are"]. When the process is completed, the chieftains take the soul out of [Purgatory] and lead it to the gate of Paradise and say to the angel messengers standing there: "*Hinnom*, behold, here is the soul that has come out pure and white" (Zohar IV, 211b).

The Jewish mystical tradition suggests that the soul's spiritual body dons an ethereal garment on entering Lower Paradise; otherwise, it must remain condemned to the torments of Purgatory.

In Lower Paradise, according to the rather materialistic vision of the Jewish sages, the spiritual body of each soul is clad in a terrestrial type of garment, albeit finer than its earthly clothes.[3] These robes, which the righteous wear, reflect their spiritual awareness and

[2]Raphael, *Afterlife*, p. 389.
[3]*Ibid.*, pp. 296–298, 309–311.

attainments while alive. The good deeds an individual performed on earth, as well as his or her kind words and generous thoughts, constitute, metaphorically speaking, the elements of garments worn by the soul's spiritual body in Lower Paradise. Sustained by these actions, as well as his or her words and thoughts, the soul's spiritual body is dressed in "garments of glory" made out of the lifetime of its good deeds and speech (Zohar IV, 210b). As the mystics teach:

> A man's good deeds done in this [material] world draw from the celestial resplendency of light a garment with which he may be invested when in the next world he comes to appear before the Holy Blessed One (Zohar IV, 229b).

Thus, when the soul enters the Lower Paradise, it "dons a likeness in the semblance of the body it tenanted in this [material] world: that likeness being, as it were, a garment with which the spirit robes itself so that there it may enjoy the delights of the radiant [Paradise]" (Zohar III, 141b).

In contrast to Lower Paradise, where the souls still find themselves in a more earthly but still spiritual type of garment, in Upper Paradise, according to the mystics, the spiritual bodies of souls are seen as attired in even more precious celestial-type garments.

THE SOUL'S RESTFUL JOURNEY IN UPPER PARADISE

The soul eventually leaves Lower Paradise and enters Upper Paradise, the realm of heavenly bliss. After the last vestiges of the deceased's personal and emotional life cease in Lower Paradise, the soul basks in the realm of Upper Paradise, a region designed for the soul's higher dimensions. In Upper Paradise the soul attains an even higher level of emotional, intellectual, and spiritual fulfillment, experiencing ecstasy as well as the joy of being close to God.

On entering Upper Paradise, the soul once again takes a dip in the heavenly River of Light and experiences a second Life Review. (These two steps were discussed, respectively, on pages 99–100 and 106–109 of Chapter 5 in connection with the Death Moment Visions.) This second immersion in the River of Light further heals the soul, purging it of any remaining impurities and impressions from its immediate past earthly existence so that it is able to perceive the glory found in Upper Paradise. According to the mystics:

> [Another] ordeal has to be undergone by the soul on its passage from Lower Paradise to Upper Paradise; for [while] in Lower Paradise it is not yet entirely purged of the materialities of this [earthly] world, so as to be fit to ascend on high. They thus pass it through the "River of [Light]," from which it emerges completely purified and so comes before the presence of the Sovereign of the universe purified in every aspect. Also, the rays of the celestial light afford it healing. This is its final stage. At this stage, the souls stand garbed in their raiment and adorned in their crowns before their Maker (Zohar IV, 211b).

In addition to a second immersion in the River of Light, the second Life Review is equally significant. The events of the deceased's life just lived and completed are once again viewed from the perspective of each immortal soul's many lifetimes. The meaning of what the deceased experienced in his or her most recent life becomes clear from the viewpoint of the soul's eternal self.

The Jewish mystics regard Upper Paradise as a world of transcendental bliss where the soul experiences the emotional, intellectual, and spiritual rewards it merits. Each righteous soul dwells in a level of Upper Paradise according to the merits of and as a reward for its deeds, words, and thoughts accumulated during its immediate past physical existence on earth. Each soul finds other kindred spirits: loving, compassionate, forgiving, noble, courageous, and humble.

Putting behind its immediate past life's desires, attachments, and

emotions and without any strife, guilt, bitterness, or competitive-
ness, in Upper Paradise each soul experiences the delight of study-
ing and meditating on the Divine harmony and mysteries of the
cosmos. Likeminded souls gather together in what the mystics
metaphorically describe as the Celestial Academy. There, each soul
attains a majestic, rather blissful understanding of God. The Eternal appears daily in the Celestial Academy and shares the Divine
wisdom with the souls who dwell there. These souls are said by
Jewish sages to derive great, almost unimaginable joy from being
close to God.

The near death experiencers studied by Raymond Moody express a new found respect for knowledge and learning, for life's
intellectual aspects. Some realize that learning doesn't end when you
die. You continue to learn and to grow. Others describe an entire
afterlife realm set aside for passionately pursuing knowledge, what
one woman described as a "big university."[4]

As intellectual aspects come to the fore, the souls, according to
the mystical tradition, passionately engage in the pursuit of knowledge in Upper Paradise. The Jewish mystics view the souls as en-
grossed in deep, ongoing conversations about the cosmos, human
existence, and universal wholeness. The souls ponder timeless questions, including the meaning and purpose of our earthly life, and
why many humans endure much pain and suffering during their
mortal lifetimes. Thus, Upper Paradise satisfies the mind.

According to the mystics, in Upper Paradise the soul uses its
newly acquired knowledge to further its personal wholeness and
human interconnectedness.[5] This knowledge allows the soul to feel
whole again in all of its aspects. The soul reflects within itself the
Wholeness that is God.

[4]Raymond A. Moody, Jr., M.D. with Paul Perry (1990), *The Light Beyond* (New York:
Bantam), p. 43.
[5]Raphael, *Afterlife*, pp. 390–391.

Each soul comes to perceive the existence of a transcendent, transpersonal awareness. Each soul gains a richer, deeper understanding of life on earth. The intellectual and spiritual maturity attained in Upper Paradise, particularly the expanded view of the world and the cosmos, permits each soul to become even more inclusive in its worldview and to acknowledge the unity of all human beings.

As it passes through Upper Paradise, each soul perceives the universe as a unified whole. Everything in the cosmos—every leaf, each cloud, and every living creature—comes to be seen as interconnected.

Perceptions of awe and wonder abound in the midst of a grand, majestic order. The distinctions between any individual soul and the infinite God gradually become blurred. Each soul lives before the Eternal, bathed in unconditional love and compassion, experiencing the glories of inner peace and spiritual fulfillment.

THE GEOGRAPHY OF PARADISE

As we did in discussing Purgatory in Chapter 7, it is helpful to visualize, however metaphorically, Paradise. Descriptions of the geography of Paradise began with the rabbinic literature, reaching their most vivid in the medieval interpretative writings.

The rabbis envisioned seven groupings of the righteous in Paradise. The righteous were seen as dwelling in the following seven different stories of Paradise, one higher than the other: the Presence (where the souls sit in God's company and behold the Divine presence); the House of God; the Mountain of God; the Court of God; the Tent of God; the Holy Hill of God; and finally, the Holy Place of God.[6]

---

[6]*The Midrash on Psalms* 11:6, trans. William G. Braude (New Haven, CT: Yale University Press, 1959).

The medieval interpretative (Midrash) writings provide the most descriptive of all Jewish writings on Paradise, a realm filled with spices, trees, angels, perfumes, and jewels. One fourteenth century author provides us with this rather stunning visual overview of Paradise:

1. When the just man approaches [the sixty myriads of ministering angels who watch over the two entrance gates] they divest him of the clothes in which he had been buried, and clothe him with eight cloths, woven out of the clouds of glory, and place upon his head two crowns, one of precious stones and pearls, and the other of gold, and they place eight myrtles in his hand and praise him, and say to him, "Go and eat [your] bread with joy." And they lead him to a place full of waters . . . surrounded by eight-hundred species of roses and myrtles. Each one has a canopy according to his merits . . . .

2. And through [Paradise] flow four rivers, one of oil, the other of balsam, the third of wine, and the fourth of honey. Every canopy is overgrown by a vine of gold, and thirty pearls hang down from it, each of them shining like the morning star.

3. In every canopy there is a table of precious stones and pearls. . . . The least fair of the [angels of the righteous] is as beautiful as Joseph [the eldest son of Jacob and Rachel] . . . and as the grains of the pomegranate lit up by the rays of the sun. And there is no night, as it is said, "And the light of the righteous is as the shining light."

. . .

5. In Paradise, there are eighty myriads of trees in every corner; the meanest among them [is] choicer than a garden of spices. In every corner there are sixty myriads of angels singing with sweet voices, and the tree of life stands in the middle

and overshadows the whole of Paradise; and it has five-hundred tastes, each different from the others, and the perfumes thereof vary likewise.

6. Over [Paradise] hangs seven clouds of glory, and the winds blow from all four corners and waft their [fragrance] from one end of the world to the other . . . . These have two canopies, one of stars and the other of sun and moon, and clouds of glory separate one from another.[7]

Within Paradise, Jewish mysticism teaches, there are seven realms for purified, righteous souls. (Perhaps you've heard the phrase: Seventh Heaven.) The more spiritually developed a soul, the higher the realm in which it dwells. Each level has accompanying angels and Biblical figures who serve as leaders of specific regions as follows:

LEVELS OF PARADISE[8]

Seventh: For: The Perfect

Angels: Holy Angels

Heads: Abraham, the founder of the Jewish people and the first Patriarch.

Isaac, the second Patriarch, the son of Abraham and Sarah.

[7]Adapted from "Paradise" in *The Chronicles of Jerahmeel*, XVII, trans. M. Gaster (New York: Ktav, 1971), pp. 40–41.

[8]Adapted from "The Garden of Eden and the World to Come," in *Revelation and Redemption: Jewish Documents of Deliverance from the Fall of Jerusalem to the Death of Nahmanides*, ed. and trans. George Wesley Buchanan (Dillsboro, NC: Western North Carolina, 1978), pp. 559–563; and Louis Ginzberg (1968), *The Legends of the Jews*, trans. Henrietta Szold (Philadelphia: Jewish Publication Society), vol. 5, pp. 32–33, n. 97.

Jacob, the third Patriarch, the son of Isaac and Rebecca.

Sarah, Abraham's wife and Isaac's mother.

Rebecca, the wife of Isaac and mother of Jacob.

Leah, the first wife of Jacob.

Rachael, the co-wife (with Leah) of Jacob.

Sixth:　For:　Schoolchildren who have not sinned

　　　Angels:　Cherubim and Metratron, the Angel of Countenance, who, according to tradition, stands face to face with God and is one of the supreme powers in the Divine realm.

　　　Head:　Joshua, Moses' aide and his successor.

Fifth:　For:　The Repentants who returned to God in a fitting manner.

　　　Angels:　Ophanim and Barkiel.

　　　Heads:　Manasseh, King of Judah during the captivity in Babylon.

　　　　　Abigail, King David's wife.

Fourth:　For:　The Holy covered by the cloud of glory

　　　Angels:　Heavenly angels

　　　Heads:　Aaron, the first high priest, who was the elder brother of Moses.

　　　　　Huldah, the prophet.

Third:　For:　The Perfect who do not entertain impure thoughts of God's ways.

　　　Angels:　Tarshishim

　　　Heads:　Eleazar, the son of Aaron.

　　　　　Miriam, the sister of Moses and Aaron, who is called a prophet.

Second:	For:	The Upright who are just in their ways and act with an upright heart and without any evil thoughts.
	Angels:	Hashmalim
	Heads:	Phineas, the son of Eleazar and the grandson of Aaron.
		Yokheved, the wife of Amram.
First:	For:	The Righteous who performed meritorious deeds, including martyrs, such as Rabbi Akiva.
	Angels:	Aralim
	Heads:	Joseph, the eldest son of Jacob and Rachel.
		Batyah, the daughter of Pharaoh, who rescued Moses and served as his foster mother.

PARADISE REFLECTS OUR CONSCIOUSNESS

For the Jewish mystics, what a soul experiences in Paradise (which it's useful to reiterate they view as a state of consciousness), directly reflects one's experiences during his or her last physical existence and his or her enduring spiritual awareness. Each soul creates its own paradise. There are, in other words, almost an infinite number of postdeath realms of consciousness.

Each soul encounters the emotional, spiritual, and intellectual bliss appropriate to its lifetime attainments. Thus, for example, according to the Jewish sages, a spiritually developed soul in the earthly realm will occupy an even higher realm of awareness in the postdeath world.

Reflecting the interconnectedness between the world of the living and what a soul experiences in Paradise, the mystics indicate that our lifetime of deeds, words, and thoughts have consequences, large and small, and impact on the destiny of each of us in the postmortem realms. The mystical writings indicate:

> For it is the path taken by man in this world that determines the path of the soul on her departure. Thus, if a man is drawn towards the Holy One, and is filled with longing toward the Eternal in this world, the soul in departing from him is carried upward towards the higher realms by the impetus given her each day in this world . . . . Rabbi Abba continued: . . . . [A]ccording to the goal which a man sets himself in this world, so does he draw to himself a spirit from on high. If he strives to attain some holy and lofty object, he draws that object from on high to himself below. But if his desire is to cleave to the other side, and he makes this his whole intent, then he draws to himself from above the other influence . . . [T]hat all depends on the kind of speech, action, and intention to which a man habituates himself, for he draws to himself here below from on high that side to which he habitually cleaves . . . [I]f a man follows a certain direction in this world, he will be led further in the same direction when he departs this world . . .: if holy, holy, and if defiled, defiled (Zohar I, 99b—100a).

The Rabbi Dov Ber—the Maggid of Mezhirich, who lived from 1704 to 1772, assuming leadership of the Hasidic movement after the Baal Shem Tov's death—put it this way:

> "A man's kind deeds are used by [God] as seed for planting of trees in [Paradise]; thus each creates his own Paradise. The reverse is true when he commits transgressions."[9]

Conceptualizing on the two aspects of Paradise, namely Lower Paradise and Upper Paradise, we see that various levels exist. Each

---

[9]*The Hasidic Anthology: Tales and Teachings of the Hasidim*, ed. and trans. Louis I. Newman (Northvale, NJ: Jason Aronson, 1987), p. 1.

soul dwells in a realm according to the accumulated merits of his or her lifetime and experiences the spiritual rewards it merits. As noted, the mystics emphasize the continuing impact of the quality and quantity of our day-to-day deeds, words, and thoughts in our worldly days.

As an individual moves from Lower Paradise to Upper Paradise, Jewish sources indicate that the quality of one's experiences in this postdeath realm continue to reflect an individual's consciousness during life. Thus, by living a more balanced, spiritually-oriented existence in the here-and-now, each of us creates beneficial experiences for our soul in the world beyond. The mystical tradition suggests these spiritually-attuned and questing souls will more easily reap the rewards of their earthly spiritual pursuits and are better able to enjoy the transcendent bliss of Upper Paradise.

According to Hasidic legend, a wicked person who enters Paradise won't enjoy its intellectual and spiritual delights. Reflecting this viewpoint, Rabbi Yakov Yosef of Polnoye—who lived from 1710 to 1784 and was perhaps the closest disciple of the Baal Shem Tov—stated:

No Purgatory can be worse for the wicked than permission to enter [Paradise]. They find there no pleasure to which they were addicted in life: no eating or drinking or any other pleasures of the body. They see merely zaddikim, deriving great pleasure from being close to [God]. And who are these zaddikim who occupy places of prominence in Paradise? They are the very persons upon whom the wicked poured out their scorn in life, and whose learning they thoroughly despised. What, then, can these persons feel in Paradise but bitterness? Can they know the joy of the Shekhinah's nearness, inasmuch as they never trained themselves in their lifetime for the enjoyments of the spirit?[10]

---

[10]*Ibid.*, p. 3.

How does the average, rather materialistically-oriented person experience his or her postmortem journey in Paradise? The following tale, offered by the Gerer Rebbe (Rabbi Yitzchak Meir Ater, who lived from 1799 to 1866), describes how a "humble" person would receive an experience in "Paradise" to which he or she could relate and enjoy:

> A *Zaddik* (a rabbi of extraordinary spiritual gifts whose cleaving to God depends on the congregation that gathered around him) was traveling in the early spring in a wagon. The roads were in terrible condition; the axles of the wheels broke several times, and the horses ploughed with difficulty through the slush and mire. Friday morning came and a great distance was yet to be covered before the *Zaddik* could reach his destination. He turned to the teamster and said: "It is important I arrive at my goal before the beginning of the Sabbath." The teamster promised to do his best. A horse fell dead from exhaustion, but the teamster continued with the second horse, and succeeded in reaching the *Zaddik's* destination before the Sabbath.
>
> On Sunday, the *Zaddik* heard that the second horse had also died from exhaustion, and that the teamster's grief was so great that he was stricken with illness. The *Zaddik* ordered the best medical attention for him, but in vain; the man died. When his soul came before the Heavenly Tribunal, the counsel for the defense won the case, and Paradise was ordered for the poor teamster. His soul arrived there, but it found no pleasure whatsoever in the spiritual and cultural atmosphere of even the lowest region. He was then sent into an imaginary world where he was presented a beautiful carriage harnessed to four magnificent horses, and where the roads stretched before him, always dry and level. The teamster was able to enjoy only an imaginary Paradise, not the true one.[11]

---

[11] *Ibid.*, p. 5.

TRADITIONAL JEWISH RITUALS

During a survivor's lifetime, two ongoing Jewish postdeath rituals exist: first, the recitation of the mourner's prayer (Kaddish) annually on the anniversary of the death of a parent or other close relative in the Hebrew calendar (the *Yahrzeit*); and second, the recitation of a memorial prayer (*Yizkor*) on four Jewish holidays.[12] These rituals are designed so that the living will never forget the dead.

Although Jews have observed the anniversary of a departed's day of death since ancient times, particularly by fasting on the anniversary of a parent's death, the term *Yahrzeit* (or year's time) originated in the medieval period. It became a time for commemorating the death of a family member or friend and for remembering their life and legacy.

On the anniversary of the death of a parent or a close relative (the *Yahrzeit*), the bereaved engage in a number of rituals, including reciting the mourner's prayer, the Kaddish (set out on pages 168–169 in Chapter 7), in the deceased's memory at the daily communal worship services held at a synagogue. If the synagogue has a memorial plaque, the decedent's name is illuminated on the day of his or her *Yahrzeit*.

On the evening before the death anniversary, a loved one also lights, at home, a *Yahrzeit* candle that burns for twenty-four hours, from sunset to sunset. This memorial candle symbolizes the departed

---

[12]For background on the laws and customs pertaining to *Yahzreit* and *Yizkor*, I have drawn on Tzvi Rabinowicz (1989), *A Guide to Life: Jewish Laws and Customs of Mourning* (Northvale, NJ: Jason Aronson), pp. 90–100; Maurice Lamm (1969), *The Jewish Way in Death and Mourning* (New York: Jonathan David), pp. 196–207; Central Conference of American Rabbis (1988), *Rabbi's Manual* (New York: Central Conference of American Rabbis), pp. 256–257; *Jewish Insights on Death and Mourning*, ed. Jack Riemer (New York: Schocken, 1995), pp. 194–220; Gershom, *Beyond the Ashes*, pp. 69–70; and Brener, *Mourning & Mitzvah*, pp. 215–228.

immortal soul. In lighting the *Yahrzeit* candle, the survivor symbolically aligns him or herself with the deceased's eternal spirit.

The *Yahrzeit* is also observed by visiting the departed's gravesite. Furthermore, loved ones perform good deeds and acts of kindness, such as making charitable contributions, in the decedent's memory in order to fulfill and promote his or her aspirations.

The *Yahrzeit* serves one simple but important function. It provides a time for the living to remember the dead. This is especially important as time passes and the memory of the departed fades. Observing a *Yahrzeit* allows an individual to remain in touch with the memory of a decedent.

The first *Yahrzeit* for mourners can be an especially powerful occasion. Signifying the end of the year of mourning, it functions as a ritual for completing the mourning process.

A special memorial or remembrance service (*Yizkor*) was likely first introduced into communal worship services during the Crusaders' massacres in the eleventh and twelfth centuries C.E., on the Day of Atonement (Yom Kippur)—although the practice of remembering the dead on Yom Kippur dates back to the fifth century of the Common Era. Jews sought atonement not only for their sins but also for those of deceased family members.

At least for the past several centuries, the bereaved privately say the *Yizkor* prayer or participate in special memorial services (*Yizkor*) at a synagogue, where a minyan is present, four times a year. In traditional rituals, the *Yizkor* services are held on: the Day of Atonement (Yom Kippur); *Shemini Atsaret*, the day between the last day of Succoth (a fall harvest festival) and *Simchat Torah* (when the annual Torah reading cycle ends and begins anew); the last day of Passover (a festival that, according to tradition, commemorates the biblical Exodus of the Jews from Egypt); and on the second day of *Shavuot* (a spring festival that, according to tradition, marks the giving of the Torah to Moses).

The seasonal cycle of four *Yizkor* services provides a context for remembering loved ones. By limiting the seasons of ongoing mourning, Jewish rituals provide a circumscribed vehicle for our remembrance and our accompanying emotional responses.

At these communal memorial services, the beloved recite various prayers, including the *Yizkor* prayer (May God Remember), in which each individual inserts the names of his or her departed relatives, including parents, grandparents, spouse, children, and other relatives. It's also become a common practice to recite the remembrance prayer on behalf of the six million Jews who perished in the Holocaust.

The special *Yizkor* prayer, included as part of the memorial service or recited by the beloved at home, is as follows:

> May God remember the soul of my dear _____, who has gone to his/her eternal rest. May his/her soul be bound up in the bond of life. May his/her rest be glorious, with the fullness of the joy in Your presence and the eternal bliss at Your right hand.[13]

By expressing reverence for the departed, the memorial service, marked by the special May God Remember prayer, provides a sacred time to honor the dead, a time for the remembrance of souls of loved ones. It enables the living to connect (and reconnect) regularly with memories of the departed, to reflect on the deceased's life and legacy, and to deal with any lingering issues of grief and mourning. The memorial service also assists the survivors in rededicating their lives on behalf of those who have passed into the world of the souls.

According to ancient custom, on the four Jewish holidays when the living recite the *Yizkor* prayer, they also light a memorial (*Yahrzeit*) candle for and make charitable contributions on behalf of the departed. The memorial candle is kindled at sundown, marking the commencement of the holiday when the *Yizkor* prayer is recited.

---

[13]Adapted from Dr. Joseph H. Hertz (1985), *The Authorised Daily Prayer Book*, rev. ed. (New York: Bloch), p. 1107.

The *Yahrzeit* and *Yizkor* rituals teach us to remember the dead. Long after a loved one dies, the Jewish tradition hopes his or her legacy lives on within us.

USING ONGOING POSTDEATH RITUALS TO FACILITATE THE SOUL'S AFTERLIFE JOURNEY

In prior chapters, I've discussed how Jewish rituals perform a soul-guiding function. I've indicated how an interactive relationship, a window of communication, exists between the world of the living and the departed soul. Let's examine the soul-guiding functions of the two postdeath rituals, *Yahrzeit* and *Yizkor*.[14]

Through the annual recitation of the Mourner's Prayer, the Kaddish, on the anniversary of a parent's (or other close relative's) death (the *Yahrzeit*), the mystical tradition suggests that the living provide a spiritual benefit for a departed soul. The merit of remembering the dead helps a deceased's soul rise to higher and higher realms of Paradise on its ongoing journey in the postdeath world. According to the Baal Shem Tov:

> A zaddik's soul does not at first ascend to the upper regions of Paradise. In the beginning he resides in [Lower Paradise], where he is still in incomplete bliss; only by degrees is he conducted to higher and higher realms. If he has left a son or a daughter or a fund of money for charity, and is remembered through the offering of a prayer and charity on the anniversary of his death, this memorial serves as an aid in the ascension of the zaddik in Paradise.[15]

---

[14]Simcha Steven Paull (1986), *Judaism's Contribution to the Psychology of Death and Dying* (Ph.D. diss., California Institute of Integral Studies), p. 371.

[15]*The Hasidic Anthology*, p. 4.

The special prayers recited during the memorial services held four times a year call on God to remember and provide merciful treatment for the deceased's soul. Thus, reciting the *Yizkor* prayer (May God Remember) at a memorial service, according to the Jewish mystics, like the *Yahrzeit* observance, helps elevate the soul of a departed loved one to an even higher level of Paradise. Saying the *Yizkor* prayer also assists in strengthening the spiritual bonds between the living and the soul of the departed. This spiritual bond, linking the past to the present, allows us to prepare for the future with hope and a sense of being connected to those we have known and loved.

An Orthodox rabbi, Barry Freundel, expresses it this way:

> . . . I would term the experience of *Yizkor* a conversation with the dead. Now, the phrase "conversations with the dead" is redolent of dark rooms and mediums in mystical outfits. But superstition and television cliches aside, we should realize that we all are part of an ongoing dialogue with the dead.
>
> Many of us who have lost loved ones continue our conversations with them even after they are dead. Frequently, particularly after the pain of separation has diminished somewhat, those who remain seek solace and guidance in conversation with those they have lost. Even if we do not do it ourselves, most of us know people who stop to talk to a deceased parent or spouse each day before going to sleep or when getting up in the morning. These conversations may consist of reports on the status of their lives, questions or requests for advice. And far from being a symptom of sanity loss, this practice of "touching base" is quite comforting and salutary, if kept within reasonable limits.
>
> Some may find the prospect of such daily conversations ridiculous and certainly not *their* style, but virtually everyone does it at some point in his life. I do not know anyone who, when attending or preparing for an important event such as a bar mitzvah or a wedding, does not

picture a lost loved one present and imagine the reaction that he or she would have. This, too, is a form of conversation with the dead. . . .

[T]he dead answer our call—not in words, but in ways that nevertheless make a difference in our lives. All of us have learned valuable lessons in morality and behavior from those to whom we were close and whom we have lost. In the best of circumstances, they were positive lessons. But even if they were negative, these lessons serve as guideposts for the way we conduct our lives and are thus also part of our continuous conversation with the dead. . . .

. . .

Yizkor is the ritual embodiment of our conversations with the dead. Our conversations with the dead provide us with guidance, help us determine where we have been right and where we have been wrong, and reconcile us with our past . . . .

Sometimes our conversations with the dead are painful, sad, and tragic. At other times, they are nostalgic and even comforting. Ultimately and perhaps unexpectedly, they are a celebration of the human capacity to transcend the limits of this life.

The Talmud tells us that no eye has ever seen the world beyond and then been permitted to come back and report what that world contains. But it is also true that some voices carry across that great divide. With *Yizkor* and our other conversations with the dead, if we listen, our ears can hear what our eyes may not see.[16]

[16]Barry Freundel, "Yizkor: The Unending Conversation" in *Jewish Insights on Death and Mourning*, pp. 194–195, 198.

In addition to the living attending a memorial service, engaging in communal worship, and offering the *Yizkor* prayer for the benefit of a soul on its postmortem journey, the memorial prayer performs another function. The survivors hope, based on mystical teachings, that attending a memorial service and reciting the *Yizkor* prayer will facilitate the intercession before God by the soul of the departed, producing various physical, spiritual, emotional, or material benefits for the living.

Remember Betsy, the newly-wed we met in Chapter 7? Two years after her mother's death, at a *Yizkor* service during Yom Kippur, Betsy prayed, asking for her mom's intercession. She and her husband desperately wanted a child but she was unable to conceive. The next Yom Kippur she came to services with a newborn daughter who looked just like her late mother.[17] Coincidence or something more significant at work?

Strengthening interconnectedness with the soul of a departed may also help the living find greater meaning and purpose in their lives. Perhaps, as Jewish sources suggest, the lessons the soul learns in Paradise may, in some form, be transmitted back to earth, helping the survivors live their lives with greater fervor and enabling them, from the viewpoint of Spiritual Judaism, to be more compassionate, more loving, and more forgiving of others.

SUGGESTIONS FOR SPIRITUAL SEEKERS

If you find communal worship services rather boring, strive to set aside time for reflection on the anniversary of the death (or the birth) of a parent (or other close relative) and, periodically, on other special occasions, such as holidays that were shared, during the year.

---

[17]Adapted from a lecture by Simcha Paull Raphael, "Jewish Views of the Afterlife," May 21, 1997.

Building on the interrelationship between the earthly world and the realm of the dead, seek to strengthen this linkage and find a continued sense of partnership in your relationship with the soul of the deceased. It's important for the survivors to reconnect not only with their feelings and memories regarding the earthly departed but also with his or her soul.

On a personal note, people who were major factors in my life continue to speak to me from the world of souls. When I've accomplished things of some value in this world, I sense the presence of my parents and their beaming faces. Recently when I officiated at a wedding ceremony, I particularly recall looking up and hearing my mother tell me, "I'm really proud of you, now."

Raymond Moody, the noted near death researcher, recounts his own first-person, rather ineffable experience of communicating with his grandma, which he calls difficult or even impossible to put into words.

Moody chose to attempt to see his beloved maternal grandmother whom he had missed in the years since her death. Although following his procedures for receiving "facilitated apparitions," including spending time in an apparition booth, a small dimly-lit room with walls painted black and gazing into a large mirror, Moody "felt not a twinge of her presence." After he "gave up" and was sitting alone in a room, his paternal grandmother "simply walked in." He knew her "through her unmistakable presence and through the many memories [they] reviewed and discussed." Moody recalls: "As soon as I realized who this woman was, a flood of memories rushed into my mind. Not all of these were good memories. In fact, many were distinctly unpleasant. Whereas my reminiscences of my maternal grandmother are positive, those of my father's mother were a different matter."

Moody then notes that as he gazed into the eyes of this apparition, "I quickly sensed that the woman who stood before me had been transformed in a very positive way. As she stood there, I felt warmth and love from her as well as empathy and compassion that surpassed my understanding. She was confidently humorous, with an air of quiet calm and joyfulness about her."

For Moody, the meeting was "completely natural." It was "in no way eerie or bizarre." It was "the most normal and satisfying interaction" he ever had with his paternal grandmother. "She was there in front of " him. Equally as startling was that he "just accepted it" and continued to talk with her. She did not appear "ghostly" or transparent. Rather, she "seemed completely solid in every respect." She appeared like any other person "except that she was surrounded by what appeared to be a light or an indentation in space, as if she were somehow set off or recessed from the rest of her physical surroundings."

As Moody recalls his encounter:

We discussed old times, specific incidents from my childhood. Throughout she reminded me of several events that I had forgotten. Also, she revealed something very personal about my family situation that came as a great surprise but in retrospect makes a great deal of sense . . . . [H]er revelation has made a great deal of difference in my life, and I feel much better for having heard this from her.

I say 'heard' in an almost literal sense. I did hear her voice clearly, the only difference being that there was a crisp, electric quality to it that seemed clearer and louder than her voice before she died. Others who'd had this experience before me described it as telepathic or 'mind to mind' communication. Mine was similar. Although most of my conversation was through the spoken word, from time to time I was immediately aware of what she was thinking, and I could tell that the same was true for her.

. . .

And how did our meeting end? I was so overwhelmed that I just said, 'Good-bye.' We acknowledged that we would be seeing each other again, and I simply walked out of the room. When I returned, she was nowhere to be seen. The apparition of my grandmother was gone.

What took place that day resulted in a healing of our relationship. For the first time in my life I can appreciate her humor and have a sense of some of the struggles she went through during her lifetime. Now I love her in a way that I didn't before the experience.

It also left me with an abiding certainty that what we call death is not the end of life.[18]

Create a sacred time and space where you can open your heart and mind to develop and maintain a genuine interconnection with beloved family members and friends who have left the world of the living. Find various techniques to achieve and strengthen the avenue of connection between the living and the dead. A symbol of remembrance, a picture, a letter, or a song, may be helpful.

Striving to remain in contact with the soul of a departed, you should spend time in unstructured personalized prayer, silent meditation, visualization, or using some special technique that helps you connect with the departed. Using the Forgiveness and Loving-kindness Mediation (or Visualization) (set out on pages 179–180 in Chapter 7), continue to send forgiving and loving thoughts to the soul on its journey in the postdeath realms.

Recall your gratitude to the deceased, what you learned from him or her. Give your bountiful thanks for what you received and

---

[18]Raymond Moody, M.D. with Paul Perry (1993), *Reunions: Visionary Encounters with Departed Loved Ones* (New York: Villard), pp. 24–28. (Moody developed a procedure for receiving "facilitated apparitions," which involves a person relaxing for several hours, telling Moody about the departed, good and bad memories, then leaving the subject for at least an hour in a small dimly-lit rom with black painted walls, resting in a comfortable chair and gazing into a mirror positioned so he or she cannot see his or her own reflection.) Hundreds of first person after-death communications are related in Bill Guggenheim and Judy Guggenheim (1996), *Hello From Heaven!: A New Field of Research, After-Death Communication Confirms That Life and Love are Eternal* (New York: Bantam).

how you were enriched, emotionally, intellectually, and spiritually.

As you open your heart to God in spontaneous, individual prayer, you hopefully will be able to reach beyond yourself. By crying out to and touching the Divine, you can seek continued compassion and mercy for the soul in its postmortem journey.

The following visualization may assist you, as others have found, in continuing to remember a deceased and aid its soul on the postdeath journey. Using this visualization, for ten to fifteen minutes on one or more special days throughout the year, will also help strengthen your interconnectedness with the soul of the departed.

Remembrance Visualization

Introductory Instructions. Create a warm, welcoming atmosphere, an environment of serenity and spaciousness for going beyond your ordinary perspective of reality. Lower the lights in your room.

Close your eyes, sit quietly, calm and relax your body. Breathe in and out normally, feeling where your breath flows into and out of your body. Adjust your breathing so that the in and out breaths are of the same length.

Feel yourself surrounded by warmth and love. With each breath, breathe in warmth. Feel the warmth nourishing you.

Take your time. There's no reason to hurry.

Visualize your departed dear one. Imagine his/her face before you. See his/her smile. Hear his/her words. Feel his/her presence. In your heart and in your mind, allow a conversation to unfold.

Ask him/her what it is like where he or she presently is.

Ask the departed to enter into a dialogue with you, telling you what he/she feels most proud of having done during his/her lifetime. Now ask what he/she feels most ashamed of. What does he/she most regret?

Ask the beloved if he/she could live his/her life again, what would be the single most important thing he/she would do differently?

Ask the departed how he/she would like to be remembered.

Focus on a specific situation that occurred between you and the deceased. Try to visualize how the departed would have wished the event to occur so he/she (or you) would have no regrets.

What still remains unspoken, unresolved? Listen. Let the radiance of his/her love be with you.

Concluding Instructions. Promise to remain in contact. Say your goodbyes, giving your beloved a big hug. Come back to the here-and-now. Take time to ease yourself back. Slowly bring your awareness back into your body. Feel yourself back in the room and open your eyes.

Also, if necessary, use the Remembrance Visualization, along with the Forgiveness and Lovingkindness Meditation (or Visualization), set out on pages 179–180, to continue to help mend a stormy past relationship with the departed and deal with unresolved issues.

Some of us need to continue to work out lingering resentments. Sending lovingkindness and forgiveness, so important in Spiritual Judaism, to the soul of a loved one often encompasses both the living and the dead in the embrace of radiant love.

Over the years, feelings with respect to the dead generally change and soften. You may be able to achieve a new rapport with the departed.

Forging a new relationship also helps heal the soul of the departed, enabling it to achieve the higher reaches of emotional, intellectual, and spiritual bliss. In reframing our memories of the past, from the perspective of Spiritual Judaism, we practice forgiveness not only for ourselves but also for the soul of a deceased loved one.

Beyond prayers, meditations, and visualizations, spiritual seekers find other special ways to memorialize and communicate with a loved one. On the anniversary of her father's death, Alexandra Kennedy, a California psychotherapist, lit a candle and played a recording of one of her dad's favorite classical music pieces, to which she danced. As she put it, "I felt the missing of him and the emptiness as I moved. Then, I felt life."[19]

You may find it useful to go outside on a starlit evening and begin a dialogue with your loved one's soul, focusing on one bright star as the symbol of your beloved. Speaking with the soul of the departed may allow years of separateness to disappear. Or, it may strengthen an existing window of communication.

Eventually, the soul completes its time in Paradise. The soul then embarks on the next stage in its postmortem journey.

---

[19]Ellen Uzelach (1994), "The Eye of Mourning," *Common Boundary* 12, no. 6 (November/December): 39, 41.

CHAPTER NINE

SPIRITUAL UNIFICATION:
RETURN TO THE SOURCE OF LIFE
AND REINCARNATION

A fter a departed soul completes its evolution in Paradise, the soul returns to the Source, the Divine Storehouse of the Souls, to prepare for rebirth in a new physical body. The soul's reincarnation in the earthly world marks the full circle of its postmortem journey. Rebirth gives a soul the opportunity to atone for any past misdeeds and actualize its potential by improving its physical, emotional, intellectual, and spiritual attributes through its thoughts, words, and behavior as a new human being on earth.

RETURN TO THE SOURCE OF LIFE

Before any soul is reborn again, it gathers together with other souls in what the Jewish tradition describes as the transcendent realm of the souls. Each soul returns to the Divine Source of all life, to the realm of being with God.[1]

---

[1]Simcha Paull Raphael (1994), *Jewish Views of the Afterlife* (Northvale, NJ: Jason

Jewish sources refer to the soul as returning on its postmortem journey to the Storehouse of Souls, the place of the origin and the termination of all souls. The Divine Treasury of Souls was often equated with the biblical bond of life, the bundle of the living (I Samuel 25:29).

The rabbis repeatedly spoke of the Divine Treasure House, a realm where righteous souls gather. The rabbis perceived this transcendent realm of souls as a postdeath gathering place, a storehouse for the righteous souls in the highest Divine spheres, where each disembodied soul prepares for earthly rebirth in a new physical body.

In the Storehouse of Souls, for those souls who have returned from completing their postmortem sojourn through Purgatory and Paradise, the mystics taught: "[T]he virtuous who are thought to be worthy to be 'bound up in the bundle of the living' are privileged to see the glory of [God], and their abode is higher than that of all the holy angels. . . . " (Zohar V, 182b). Recall also the *Yizkor* Memorial Prayer (May God Remember) in Chapter 8, which asks that the departed soul be "bound up in the bond of life."

REINCARNATION: THE SOUL'S REBIRTH IN A NEW PHYSICAL BODY

Although the concept of reincarnation fires the modern mind, it remains a challenge for empirical proof. However, some intriguing evidence exists. Ian Stevenson, M.D., a professor of psychiatry, has spent his professional career investigating cases of young children, especially in India, who spontaneously recall past lives.

Aronson), pp. 154–156, 313–314, 392; Gershom Scholem (1991), *On the Mystical Shape of the Godhead: Basic Concepts in the Kabbalah*, ed. Jonathan Chipman, trans. Joachim Neugroschel (New York: Schocken), p. 205.

Stevenson has documented more than 2,600 cases suggestive of reincarnation. These children, when brought into contact with their families from prior lives, recognized siblings and parents without any prompting. Stevenson also found examples in which birthmarks in this life correspond to wounds inflicted on the body in previous earthly existences.[2]

Evidence of reincarnation also comes as a result of past life regression under hypnosis. In his best selling book, *Many Lives, Many Masters*,[3] psychiatrist Brian L. Weiss, M.D., tells the story of Catherine, a young laboratory technician who came into his office complaining of chronic fears of water, choking, darkness, and dying. After a year marked by lack of success with conventional psychotherapy, Weiss encouraged her to try hypnosis. After several sessions, he instructed her to go back to the time when her symptoms first arose. Catherine described herself as a young woman living in 1863 B.C.E. She recalled a tidal wave destroying her village. As Catherine revealed more of her past lives, more of her symptoms subsided.

Leaving these modern case studies, the belief in the Jewish tradition that a departed soul enters a new body is found neither in the Bible nor in the rabbinic literature. Rather, the Jewish mystics, beginning with the *Zohar* (the *Book of Splendor*, a major mystical text, which modern scholarship dates to the thirteenth century C.E.), speak of reincarnation (*gilgul* in Hebrew) as marking the rebirth of the soul and its reentry into a new physical body.

---

[2]Ian Stevenson, M.D. (1981), *Twenty Cases Suggestive of Reincarnation*, rev. ed. (Charlottesville, VA: University Press of Virginia); and Ian Stevenson, M.D. (1987), *Children Who Remember Past Lives: A Question of Reincarnation* (Charlottesville, VA: University Press of Virginia). The evidence in support of the concept of reincarnation is summarized in Liz Hodgkinson (1989), *Reincarnation: The Evidence* (London: Piatkus).

[3]Brian L. Weiss, M.D. (1988), *Many Lives, Many Masters* (New York: Simon and Schuster).

Building on kabbalistic thought, reincarnation plays a central role among Hasidic Jews. The Baal Shem Tov proclaimed himself to be a reincarnation of Rabbi Saadia Gaon—the first eminent philosopher of medieval Judaism, who lived from 882 to 942 C.E.[4]

Rabbi Levi Issac of Berdichev, affectionately known as the Berdichever Rabbe—who lived from 1740 to 1810 and was one of the towering Hasidic figures—was said to be a reincarnation of Rabbi Akiba.[5] (Rabbi Akiba was one of the ten righteous ones martyred by the Romans at the time of the Bar Kokba revolt, the second Jewish revolt against the Romans (132–135 C.E.). He laid the foundations for the exposition of biblical interpretations later codified in the Mishnah, which today comprises part of the Talmud.)

A story is also told concerning Rabbi Abraham Joshua Heschel of Apt, the Apter Rav, who lived from 1755 to 1825, and claimed he had been in the world ten times. During the historical portion of the synagogue service on Yom Kippur afternoon, when reading the liturgy about the High Priest of the Temple in Jerusalem, the Apter Rebbe would say: "Thus did I say." Not, "Thus did he say."[6]

But what purpose does reincarnation serve in the Jewish tradition? Through rebirth, a soul can improve its good deeds, words, and thoughts, perhaps remedying any wrongdoing committed in its immediate past life. The soul can also attain further physical, emotional, intellectual, and spiritual purification, completing its tasks, which vary from person-to-person, before reaching its ultimate destination, union with God, discussed later in this chapter. In ad-

---

[4]*In Praise of the Baal Shem Tov: The Earliest Collection of Legends About the Founder of Hasidism*, trans. and ed. Dan Ben-Amos and Jerome R. Mintz (Northvale, NJ: Jason Aronson, 1993), pp. 106–107.

[5]Jerome R. Mintz (1968), *Legends of the Hasidim: An Introduction to Hasidic Culture and Oral Tradition in the New World* (Chicago: University of Chicago Press), p. 93.

[6]Mintz, *Legends*, pp. 93, 182; and Gedalyah Nigal (1994), *Magic, Mysticism, and Hasidism: The Supernatural in Jewish Thought*, trans. Edward Levin (Northvale, NJ: Jason Aronson), pp. 52–53, 238, n. 11.

dition to striving to attain perfection for its own benefit, rebirth also affords a righteous soul the opportunity to provide others with love and compassion and generally, to be of selfless service to humanity.

The mother of an infant girl who died in her sleep at less than three months old—a tragic, unexplained, sudden infant death—recounted the following Hasidic story told to her as one to whom a special soul had been sent for only a short stay to mend itself, thereby making the experience spiritually meaningful:

> [A] baby [was] born to a loving, fine Jewish woman, who lived two years and died suddenly. The mother went to the rebbe who had given her the blessing for the child, and he told her a strange story of a certain Jew who grew up to be an outstanding member of the community who, unfortunately, had been lost among other nations for several years during his youth. It was only through a special spark that this unique soul possessed that it was able to renounce its foreign background and return to Judaism. The story tells us that when this soul was reunited with its Maker after 120 years, God felt that the soul, as wonderful as were the deeds it had achieved on earth, lacked one thing. For two years it had been nursed by a stranger. So the special, beautiful soul had to return to earth, to a fine, caring Jewish mother, for two years. And this soul was her baby, the one that had lived two years and died.[7]

Another Hasidic tale aptly illustrates the significance of humility, an important attribute of our conduct towards others, and suggests that an individual may be reborn to atone for even one "bad" deed, word, or thought in his or her immediate past life:

> On a certain New Year's night, the Maggid of Zlotchov (Rabbi Yechiel Michel of Zlotchov, a Hasidic rabbi who lived from 1721 to 1786) saw

---

[7]Rookie Billet (1995), "We Will Get Better, We Must Get Better" in *Jewish Insights on Death and Mourning*, ed. Jack Riemer (New York: Schocken), p. 289.

a man who had been a reader in his city and who had died a short time ago. "What are you doing here?" he asked.

"The rabbi knows," said the dead man "that in this night, souls are incarnated anew. I am such a soul."

"And why were you sent out again?" asked the Maggid.

"I led an impeccable life here on earth," the dead man told him.

"And yet you are forced to live once more?" the Maggid went on to ask.

"Before my death," said the man, "I thought over everything I had done and found that I had always acted in just the right way. Because of this my heart swelled with satisfaction and in the midst of this feeling I died. So now they have sent me back into the world to atone for my pride."

At that time a son was born to the Maggid. His name was Rabbi Wolf [of Zbarazh]. He was very humble.[8]

REINCARNATION: SOME FURTHER DETAILS

Jewish sages wondered through the ages, who is reincarnated?[9] Initially, Jewish mystics believed that only those guilty of certain sexual sins as well as married couples who did not conceive children or those who did not marry were reincarnated.[10] In these situations,

[8]Martin Buber (1975), *Tales of the Hasidim: The Early Masters*, trans. Olga Marx (New York, Schocken), p. 158.

[9]I have drawn from Raphael, *Afterlife*, pp. 314–320, 392–394; Scholem, *Godhead*, pp. 197–250; David A. Cooper (1997), *God is a Verb: Kabbalah and the Practice of Mystical Judaism* (New York: Riverhead), pp. 117–120, 265–269; Rifat Sonsino and Daniel B. Syme (1990), *What Happens After I Die? Jewish Views of Life After Death* (New York: UAHC Press) pp. 46–53; Yonassan Gershom (1992), *Beyond the Ashes: Cases of Reincarnation from the Holocaust* (Virginia Beach, VA: A.R.E. Press), pp. 70–80, 196–205; and Gershon Winkler (1982), *The Soul of the Matter: A Psychological and Philosophical Study of the Jewish Perspective on the Odyssey of the Human Soul Before, During, and After "Life"* (New York: The Judaica Press), pp. 17–19.

[10]Scholem, *Godhead*, p. 209–211.

the mystics maintained that reincarnation served to administer God's retributive punishment.

Through rebirth, a soul would receive another lifetime as a Divine gift, to make good where it had failed to fulfill its prior destiny or make amends for its prior sins. Of particular importance was child rearing, which the mystics viewed as a key aspect of our existence on this planet. No one could pass beyond the earthly realm before having raised, during a lifetime, at least one child to adulthood.

With the passage of time, the Jewish mystics first viewed reincarnation as open just to evil doers, and subsequently, to evil doers, ordinary or middling people, and the righteous. Also, through reincarnation, a perfectly righteous person could help other humans attain a higher degree of spiritual perfection.

Beyond the general notion of reincarnation, the details remain quite fuzzy. The Jewish mystics were (and they are) unable to agree on a number of tantalizing details, including who comes back and the length of time between incarnations. The number of times a soul comes back varied, according to Jewish sages, from four incarnations for righteous souls all the way up to one hundred or even a thousand rebirths for a wicked soul.[11] Seemingly, no limit exists on the number of reincarnations for the righteous whose souls are reborn for the good of the entire world.

Disputes also focused on when the soul is implanted in a new physical body. The range of possibilities include: at conception, forty days after conception, just before or at the moment of birth, or even up to five days after birth. According to one strand of the rabbinic materials, for the first forty days after conception, the fetus is mere fluid in the womb. (Talmud, *Yevamoth* 69b). In other places, the Talmud indicates that a fetus in the womb is not an independent person, presumably because it lacks a soul. (*Arakhin* 7a; *Sanhedrin*

---

[11]*Ibid.*, p. 201, 211; Nigal, *Magic*, pp. 53, 238–239, n. 12; Gershom, *Beyond the Ashes*, pp. 76, 196–197.

76b). Thus, a fetus only becomes a person when its head or the greater part of its body emerges at birth.

Finally, it's unclear whether an individual is reborn as the same or the opposite sex. Infertility was explained by Jewish mystics as resulting from the exchange of souls during reincarnation. A male soul born in a female body (or a female soul in a male body) will make the bearer barren.[12]

Some Jewish mystics espoused the concept of transmigration, a notion basic to the Eastern religious traditions. Transmigration connotes that an individual guilty of grave transgressions might be incarnated on earth as an animal, particularly a chicken, a dog, a plant, a flower, or even an inanimate object, such as a stone.[13]

A number of Hasidic tales illustrate the corrective powers of a transmigration. One story was told about Rabbi Meshullam Zisha of Hanipol (who lived from 1718 to 1800 and was the younger brother of Rabbi Elimelech of Lizhensk) as he travelled with his servant. On their way, they saw some birds striking a tree with their beaks. Rabbi Zisha indicated that a transmigrated soul was in the tree and that the soul had made its correction.[14]

Through transmigration into a fish, a soul could obtain its correction, especially if eaten by a righteous person. According to one tale, Rabbi Simcha Bunim of Przysucha (who lived from 1767 to 1827) once went to a river and saw a large fish that threw itself on a boat. Reb Bunim indicated, "I took the fish and affected its correction [by] myself, conducting over it *Kol Nidrei*."[15]

Another story is told of Rabbi Joseph, the father of Rabbi Yudel of Chudnor. Rabbi Joseph appeared to his son in a dream one Friday evening. He revealed to his son that he had reincarnated into a

---

[12]Scholem, *Godhead*, p. 221.

[13]Nigal, *Magic*, pp. 55–62; Raphael, *Afterlife*, pp. 318–319; Winkler, *Soul*, pp. 21–22.

[14]Nigal, *Magic*, pp. 55–56.

[15]*Ibid.*, p. 58.

large fish that a righteous person purchased for consumption on Shabbat.[16]

However, most Jewish mystics reached the conclusion that souls are reborn again only as human beings. Their reasoning is quite simple. Only rebirth as a human enables a soul to continue its process of evolution and purification.

Despite these quibbles, one thing is clear. The Jewish tradition indicates that only a very few souls do not require reincarnation.

REINCARNATION: A REALITY CHECK

If we undergo reincarnation, why don't most of us remember our past lives? One explanation is found in a medieval text describing how a soul prepares for its rebirth into the earthly world. According to this writer, two angels are said to accompany the soul before it is placed in the womb or when it is in the womb. A light set above the soul enables the soul to see from one end of the world to the other. One angel accompanies the soul to Paradise to see the fate of righteous souls. Then, the soul is shown the fate of the wicked in Purgatory. The soul is briefed, receiving a preview of his or her coming life, including where it will reside, die, and be buried. This author continues:

> When the time arrives for [the soul] to emerge from the womb into the open world, [an] angel addresses the soul, "The time has come for you to go [forth] into the open world." The soul demurs, "Why [do you] want to make me go forth into the open world?" The angel replies: "Know that as [you were] formed against [your] will, so now [you will] be born against [your] will, and against [your] will [you shall] die, and against [your] will give account of [yourself] before the [Blessed

---

[16]*Ibid.*, p. 59.

Holy One]." But the soul is reluctant to leave her place. The angel [touches] the babe on the nose, extinguishes the light at his head, and brings him forth into the world against his will. Immediately the child forgets all his soul has seen and [learned], and he comes into the world crying, for he loses a place of shelter and security and rest.[17]

But why don't most of us remember our past lives? There's a ring of logic to our present amnesia. Each of us has a role to play in earthly life, here and now. Knowledge about our past might, therefore, interfere with our current role as well as our free will. According to one researcher of past life regression through hypnosis, "This amnesia is invaluable in that it prevents endless pining and homesickness for the grandeur that has been left behind and allows the individual to embark on the new life unhindered by confusing echoes of past deeds and misdeeds."[18]

What the soul retains, perhaps, are those enduring lessons and truths of significance for its physical, emotional, intellectual, and spiritual evolution in its present incarnation. Most of us cannot recall specific information, whether our past identity or the names of people we knew in past lifetimes, or dates, or places. The positive lessons and truths, the wisdom but not the details, the soul previously learned hopefully will be used for the benefit of not only one individual, but also, more generally, for humanity. However, some individuals are able to recall specifics of one or more past lives, particularly through past-life regression analysis under hypnosis. One of a number of Holocaust reincarnation case histories collected by Rabbi Yonassan

[17]*Legends of the Jews*, ed. Louis Ginzburg and trans. Henrietta Szold (Philadelphia: Jewish Publication Society, 1968), vol. 1, pp. 58–59; "The Formation of the Child" in *The Chronicles of Jerahmeel* IX: 8, trans. M. Gaster (New York: Ktav, 1971), p. 21.

[18]Joel L. Whitton, M.D., Ph.D. and Joe Fisher (1986), *Life Between Life: Scientific Explorations into the Void Separating One Incarnation from the Next* (Garden City, NY: Doubleday), p. 49.

Gershom, involves a baby boomer, Abbye Silverstein, born on March 10, 1953 to Jewish working-class parents in the Bronx, New York. Abbye recalls:

> . . . [M]y home was an emotional and spiritual desert. This was due to the death of my maternal grandfather just before my birth, and the death of his entire family in Russia during the Holocaust. Because of these recent tragedies, there was no warmth on a daily basis in our house; our communications concerned everyday routine functions. My family was unconsciously mourning, but how could a child know that? I would reach out to hug my parents and grandmother, and they would appease me—sometimes. It was as if everyone lived in his or her own separate rooms, not wanting to be disturbed. I felt like I didn't belong to this family, like a stranger in a strange land, and I longed for *my own* family. . . . So I found my solace by meditating and praying. . . .

> . . .

> At the age of seven, I watched my first Holocaust documentary on PBS and cried uncontrollably. My mother joked about this, saying that I cried as if I had been there. But to me, it was no joke. In my mind, a voice answered, "Yes, I was there."

> Plus there were other flashbacks or "bleed-throughs" that I couldn't explain. I was deeply disturbed by the sight of a Mercedes-Benz dealership on Boston Post Road and would be filled with fear when riding in a fast car on winding roads. . . .

> I would often flash back on a dark-haired bearded man, feeling as if he had had a great love affair with me. For many years in this life, I searched for him in every male–female relationship that I had. I longed for his love, his presence, his mind, and his heart. It was not until he later appeared to me on the astral plane that I finally found him again in this life.

> . . .

At the age of twenty, while I was in college, I had an abortion. After the abortion, I went home to rest and had a puzzling dream:

> I was dressed in 1930s garb, walking away from a college campus filled with Gothic-style buildings. I turned back toward the campus, looked at one particular building with large stained-glass windows, and said goodbye for the last time. Then I walked toward a black Mercedes-Benz with a dark-haired, bearded man in the driver's seat. Again, I looked back to say goodbye. We drove away, and the word *DEATH* appeared before me.

I awoke feeling very disturbed. But I would not understand this dream until much later, when my first past-life regression revealed the memories that I had stored within my higher self. . . .

. . .

On the weekend of December 1–3, 1978, my prayers were answered with a series of psychic dreams. The final dream revealed the initial clue which led to my first past-life regression:

> A dark-haired, bearded man appeared to me, dressed in modern-day clothing. He identified himself as Richard (pronounced as in German: ree-KHARD) and gave me this message: "You and I were lovers. We were married in a past life and died together. We have come back to be together again, to continue the work we started. It will be soon."

I realized that the man in this dream was the same dark-haired man I had been dreaming about all my life! But over the next few months, my focus was on more earthly concerns: my separation, divorce, and getting my life in order. Then one day in July 1979, I came home from work to meditate, and, while meditating, I met the astral projection of the dark-haired man from my dream in December. I had mixed feelings about this meeting. My ego was shocked and angry that he had invaded my space, while my higher self was delighted to be reunited with him once more.

At the same time, I thought for sure that I must be going crazy, so I confided in some friends who were well versed in psychic phenomena. They all agreed that I needed to have a past-life regression, because I had "unfinished business" with this man from my last incarnation. Two days later, I was hypnotized by a professional who specialized in this type of work. The story which I now share emerged in stages, through a series of regression sessions. Putting the pieces together has helped me understand the "bleed-throughs" between my current and past lives.

. . .

In my Holocaust life, I was Anna, a German Jewish woman who grew up in the working-class section of Berlin with her mother, father, and younger sister. We were a close-knit, traditional family, with much love and warmth. *Shabbos* was celebrated weekly by the entire clan—grandparents, uncles, aunts, and cousins—who ate, prayed, and sang together.

Anna was very pretty, yet she viewed her physical beauty as secondary to her intellectual prowess. She aspired to become a psychiatrist and attended the University of Heidelberg where she met her husband, Richard. He had been raised in an upper-class, Reform Jewish family, who did not approve of Anna. But Richard married her anyway, against his father's wishes. Anna and Richard were true soul mates, perfectly matched physically, emotionally, mentally, and spiritually. Nothing could keep them apart.

At the university, they shared the same passion and purpose in life— to raise consciousness and improve humanity. He was driven by politics and law, and she by psychology and medicine. Caught up in the history of their time, Richard became involved in a student dissident group on campus.

In the spring of 1933, Anna had a miscarriage, and Hitler won the election. The Brown Shirts were now after the dissidents. Richard insisted that he and Anna should leave the country and go to England for safety, because many of their friends had already been beaten up and harassed. So Anna closed their affairs with the university and packed their belongings to escape to England.

As they drove through the forest enroute to France, Richard became enraged at the ignorance of the German people for believing in Hitler. He was also angry about his own father's denial of the political situation and the loss of his friends, his dreams, and his future. Richard seemed out of control, and Anna was frightened and helpless. She begged him to slow down as he drove at breakneck speed on the winding roads in the dark forest. There was a long stretch of silence between them. Suddenly, at a curve in the road directly ahead of the car, they saw a large, imposing tree . . .

The next thing Anna knew, her spirit had left her body, and she was dead. So was Richard. They stood there together in the spirit, viewing their own corpses. The car had crashed into a tree, and Richard's chest had been crushed against the steering wheel. Anna had fallen forward into the windshield.

Anna exclaimed, "We're *dead*! We're *dead*! Only the body dies. Consciousness never dies! Consciousness lives forever!" Then she looked at Richard and asked "Why did you do this?"

Solemnly he replied, "I had a vision. I heard a voice telling me to come with them. That they would save us. Then I saw soldiers coming to take us away. We were separated by barbed wire. I knew that one of us would live and the other would die. I couldn't bear to be separated from you . . . and the next thing I saw was the tree. I couldn't stop the car soon enough. Anna, please forgive me. But it is better to die by the hands of love than by the hands of hate."

Anna forgave Richard. They remained earthbound in the German countryside and met other discarnate spirits who were also in limbo like themselves. One day, they saw soldiers (still in the flesh) marching on the road and heard gunshots in the distance. They went to investigate and found the bodies of dead Jews in a large open pit or grave. Anna screamed, "They're killing us! They're killing the Jews! Richard, you were right—you saved us!"

Of course, he had not saved them from death. But he had saved them from the horrible humiliation of being tortured by the Nazis just because they were Jews. Richard replied, "Anna, now you understand that it is better to die by the hands of love than by the hands of hate." At that moment, they heard a Voice calling to them. The time had come to transcend the earth plane. White-golden light appeared, showing them the way to the in-between life.

In the spirit world, they were welcomed by a guard standing beside a large door. He walked them to a reception table in the Great Hall. A woman there welcomed them and explained that they were going to continue their lives in this world now. She told them that they were in training to help others. They had been spared the horrors of the Holocaust in order to be of service to the victims. They were sent to heavenly classes, where they studied with the great Jewish masters about religion, philosophy, psychology, and the psychic healing of the soul.

Anna's first assignment in the spirit world was as an intake worker. On the earth below, the Jews were being exterminated, and souls were entering the in-between world at a very rapid rate. She was placed in the Great Hall, which was like the "Ellis Island" of Heaven, run by the "United Jewish Appeal" [an umbrella funding agency for Jewish organizations] of the in-between world. The Jewish souls came in droves, with their astral bodies crippled and mangled with torture, degraded, and stripped of their dignity.

As an intake worker, Anna took their vital statistics for the Akashic [life history] Record: name, place of birth, residence, occupation, family history, manner of death, etc. Soon she met her mother, father, sister, and best friend as they stood in line to check in. They had died in the Holocaust. Like the rest of the Jews, they were sent to a section of the afterworld that was designated "for Jews only"—not to segregate them, but to provide a place where their wounded spirits could heal in an atmosphere of safety.

This Jewish part of Heaven was divided into countries, cities, villages, and towns, which paralleled their homes on earth. Bulletin boards were created according to geographical regions, which posted messages for the incoming souls to find their relatives. Maps and signposts aided them in going home. Everything that had been left behind on the material plane was recreated in the spirit world in order to help these severely wounded souls make the transition toward reincarnating as the Baby Boom generation. There was a great deal of work to do in a very short period of time.

Anna was happy in the in-between world, and her life was very productive. She was "promoted" several times, until she was the supervisor of a type of healing center. As such, she attended a council of healing center administrators, to share ideas for healing and helping these Holocaust souls make the transition.

When the war ended in 1945, the Jewish section was opened up, and people were able to travel to other parts of the in-between world. Anna's husband, Richard, was preparing to reincarnate again, to be among the first wave of Baby Boomers. Anna, on the other hand, did not want to leave. Richard promised that they would find each other someday, then bid her goodbye. Anna grieved the loss of her husband, but felt content to remain in the in-between world. She realized that life is a continuum and she did not want to accept the restrictions of a physical body.

Nevertheless, by 1950 Anna could not hold out any longer. The time had come for her to be reincarnated again, but her designated mother had a miscarriage. Anna was relieved, because she wasn't ready to return yet. Three years later, she was told that she would have to enter the womb and attach to the embryo at the moment of conception, rather than wait until birth, because her mother had a fibroid tumor. By entering the womb at conception, Anna would ensure that the fetus survived to become her new body.

Reluctantly, Anna agreed. With the help of her two spirit guides, Ruth and Isaac, she wrote the contract for her new life on earth. The first forty years would be filled with struggle, physical and emotional pain, mental and spiritual challenges, learning, and the repaying of karmic debt. After this period, she would prosper materially and be able to serve God as a healer once more. Her guides promised that they would remain active in her life, providing the opening for her to remain connected to the spiritual worlds.

Anna then entered the dark womb, but stayed in a meditative trance, connected to the spirit world by a ray of white light. She remained in this meditative state until her birth on March 10, 1953, at 3:25 A.M. At that moment, the ray of light was severed, and Anna was born into the material world as Abbye Silverstein.[19]

REINCARNATION WITHIN THE LARGER SCHEME OF THINGS: HELPING ANSWER SOME DIFFICULT QUESTIONS

Reincarnation may help explain the apparent "injustices" we observe in the world. We've all asked at one time or another: Why do seemingly "good" people suffer physical or emotional pain and adversity during their lifetimes? Some of us have experienced the randomness of "fate." Others have suffered various types of rejection because of their appearance or their accent. Some have lived a life of fear. Why?

Many of us are aware of the tragic and seemingly meaningless deaths of teenagers in auto accidents. Or Jenny, a 3-year-old, stand-

---

[19]Abbye Silverstein, "The Healer Heals Herself," in Yonassan Gershom (1996), *From Ashes to Healing: Mystical Encounters with the Holocaust* (Virginia Beach, VA: A.R.E. Press), pp. 2–10.

ing a mere 3 1/2 feet tall, weighing barely 50 pounds, missing almost all the hair on her head. Suffering from cancer, she sat in the hall crying to anyone who passed by. Slowly decaying in her bed, she became too sick to be bathed. Before her death, Jenny's body resembled that of an old woman.

Yet from the perspective of the Jewish tradition, good ultimately wins out. A "good" person may suffer in this world as a consequence of words spoken or acts committed in a past incarnation. We can't escape our past but we can, however, change the results by what we do now.

Souls are reborn to be presented with and afforded the opportunity to meet and deal with new and often quite difficult challenges. In facing these challenges and the learning experiences it encounters, each soul evolves, is further purified, and fulfills its spiritual potential.

As we've seen, there's also another realm, according to the Jewish tradition, where everything gets straightened out. Justice may be delayed but it ultimately arrives. The righteous who suffer in this world will enter into the bliss of Paradise. The earthly pleasures of the wicked are transitory, leading them on the path to Purgatory.

Before expanding our discussion and putting reincarnation within this larger context, it's helpful to see how a specific soul and a particular fetus are matched. In the Storehouse of the Souls, discussed earlier in this chapter, each soul is viewed as receiving its assignment for its next incarnation. One medieval text, which portrays the soul as entering the fetus immediately after conception, explains the matching process as follows:

> The soul and body of man are united in this way: When a woman has conceived, the Angel of the Night, Lailah, carries the sperm before God, and God decrees what manner of human being shall become of it—whether it shall be male or female, strong or weak, rich or poor, beautiful or ugly, long or short, fat or thin, and what all its other

qualities shall be. Piety and wickedness alone are left to the determination of man himself. Then God makes a sign to the angel appointed over the souls, saying, "Bring Me the soul so-and-so, which is hidden in Paradise, whose name is so-and-so, and whose form is so-and-so." The angel brings the designated soul, and she bows down when she appears in the presence of God, and prostrates herself before the Eternal. At that moment, God issues the command, "Enter this sperm." The soul opens her mouth, and pleads: "O Sovereign of the world! I am well pleased with the world in which I have been living since the day on which You [did] call me into being. Why [do] You now desire to have me enter this impure sperm, I who am holy and pure, and a part of Your glory?" God consoles her: "The world which I shall cause you to enter is better than the world in which you have lived . . . , and when I created you, it was only for this purpose." The soul is then forced to enter the sperm against her will, and the angel carries her back to the womb of the mother.[20]

In the Jewish tradition, the soul's next earthly incarnation involves a mixture of God's control, Divine providence and mercy, as well as human free will. Charting the soul's future course, the mystics suggest, God tells each soul, particularly less developed souls, what its mission will be and how to fulfill it.[21] The soul receives its bodily traits, the circumstances it will encounter, and obtains its instructions and the specific lessons it needs to learn to achieve a higher degree of perfection. A soul may be assigned a spirit guide, as Anna/Abbye was. More advanced souls may only receive a general outline of their next incarnation. Each soul is reborn with the task of mending itself and also helping perfect the world.

---

[20]*Legends of the Jews*, vol. 1, pp. 56–57; "The Formation of the Child" in *The Chronicles of Jerahmeel* IX: 1–4, pp. 19–20.
[21]Whitton and Fisher, *Life Between Life*, p. 42.

Incarnations may be more difficult as the soul evolves. An impaired physical body, a difficult interpersonal relationship, or grinding poverty, to take but three examples, all serve a purpose in the Divine plan. Our life circumstances help us develop our souls.

At the same time, the Jewish tradition insists on free will. You are free to respond to the circumstances in which you find yourself, how you perceive and experience them, how you interpret what happens to you, and the choices you make in life. Using your creative imagination and your constructive will, you are responsible for who you are and what you make of your life.

Through your mind and your way of thinking, you create the world you see. How you interpret what happens to you determines your inner peace (or lack of it). Thus, for each of us, our future is not made in the womb or at birth, rather it is within our will to create it, subject, of course, to certain parameters.

In the midst of this rather uneasy balance between Divine control over our lives and our free will, it is important to realize that profound reasons exist for our being and what happens to us in our earthly sojourn, although we may be unable to discern them. Each experience contains a lesson; every relationship has its lesson; each task presents a lesson.

There are no accidents in God's plan for you. Each situation provides a means for you to become more aware of God's presence and love. A time of challenge and difficulty offers an opportunity to discover (or rediscover) your own deeper spiritual meaning.

God sends us a vast array of experiences: the people we meet; the relationships we form; the physical and emotional pain and suffering we encounter; and the other adversities we face, as learning opportunities, often quite difficult and demanding, designed to help us grow spiritually and to purify and perfect ourselves. In particular, free will is given us, from the viewpoint of Spiritual Judaism, to love and forgive others and make choices benefitting humanity.

Let's take two examples illustrating perspectives on life and death from the viewpoint of the survivors. Parents of young children who die from incurable cancer or inoperable heart defects, to take two tragic situations, have related to me that even while dying their child was their teacher. For many of these parents, the traditional role of parent and teacher was reversed. Recall Jenny, the 3-year-old mentioned earlier in this chapter. Her loving spirit continues as a comforting presence in her parents' hearts. They feel a continuation of an ongoing relationship with her. She still inspires them to live more fully and make spiritual contributions through selfless service to others.

The author of one of the leading books on death education and simple burial tells about his mother, a lovely woman, who died from typhoid fever when he was a few months old. He and his father went to live with his father's parents. His father's oldest sister became the boy's foster mother for the first six years of his life. Bereft of his wife, his father directed most of his affection to his son. Making grief a creative lifeforce, his father became a more caring, warmer person.[22]

Feeling the pain of death, the living can reach out and grow from their experience with grief and suffering. You need to ponder: How do you respond to tragic events and environments? Are you able to go beyond and surmount them? Or will you be defeated?

Overcoming life's challenges offers each of us innumerable opportunities for growth and improvement, particularly for expressing unconditional love and forgiveness. Hopefully, the soul of each of us, during its current incarnation, will evolve in one or more of the four dimensions presented in Chapter 3: physical (our actions), emotional (our words), intellectual (our thoughts), or spiritual.

---

[22]Ernest Morgan (1990), *Dealing Creatively with Death: A Manual of Death Education and Simple Burial*, twelfth rev. ed., ed. Jennifer Morgan (Bayside, NY: Barclay House), p. 31.

Constructive responses to life's vicissitudes, hardships, and learning experiences heighten the soul's consciousness and awareness, enhancing its spiritual development and thereby enabling each of us, through successive incarnations, to come closer to God. Remember that through your mind and your way of thinking, you find meaning in life and create your own future, based on your method of facing the present and the future. Many times, as you must realize, this is quite difficult.

The late Viktor E. Frankl, the renowned existential psychiatrist, tells of one of his patients, a rabbi from Eastern Europe and Holocaust survivor, who lost his first wife and six children at Auschwitz and whose second wife was sterile. The rabbi, as an Orthodox Jew, despaired that he would have no son to say Kaddish for him after his death. Frankl persisted:

> I made a last attempt to help him by inquiring whether he did not hope to see his children again in Heaven. However, my question was followed by an outburst of tears, and now the true reason for his despair came to the fore: he explained that his children, since they died as innocent martyrs [for the sanctification of God's name], were thus found worthy of the highest place in Heaven, but as for himself he could not expect, as an old, sinful man, to be assigned the same place. I did not give up but retorted, "Is it not conceivable, Rabbi, that precisely this was the meaning of your surviving your children: that you may be purified through these years of suffering, so that finally you, too, though not innocent like your children, may *become* worthy of joining them in Heaven? Is it not written in the Psalms that God preserves all your tears? [Psalm 56:9] So perhaps none of your sufferings were in vain." For the first time in many years he found relief from his suffering through the new point of view which I was able to open up to him.[23]

---

[23]Viktor E. Frankl (1984), *Man's Search for Meaning* (New York: Washington Square Press), pp. 142–143.

The experiences we encounter as reborn souls in the earthly realm serve a vital purpose in the larger scheme of things. As an educational process, these interactions give meaning and purpose to our lives and hopefully reinforce our perception of an enduring spiritual reality.

In short, reincarnation may help explain in a believable way life's seeming injustices and turns of fate that are otherwise inexplicable within the framework of a single lifetime. All of our earthly pain and suffering remind us of the impermanence of our present material existence. Also, by constructively meeting life's challenges, each of us derives positive spiritual benefits from our soul's ongoing journey in this world and the postmortem realms.

CONNECTIONS BETWEEN THE LIVING AND A DEPARTED SOUL APART FROM REBIRTH: BENIGN AND EVIL POSSESSIONS

Not all souls, however, enter a new physical body, either at the conception of a fetus, later during the pregnancy, or at the moment of birth (or shortly thereafter). Some departed souls remain in contact with souls of the living. According to the mystical tradition and Jewish folklore, lingering and clinging connections occur in the form of both benign and evil possessions.[24]

In a benign possession, according to the mystics, a living person receives a second soul which is impregnated or incorporated within his or her soul. This additional soul may accompany the person until death or it may, of its own accord, depart earlier. The duration of the stay was thought to depend on the behavior, words, or thoughts of the possessed.

---

[24]I have drawn from Raphael, *Afterlife*, pp. 321–324; Nigal, *Magic*, pp. 67–107; Winkler, *Soul*, pp. 20–21, 23, 49–65; Gershom, *Beyond the Ashes*, p. 76; Brener, *Mourning & Mitzvah*, pp. 200–202; Sonsino and Syme, *What Happens*, pp. 48–50.

A benign possession usually occurs for a good purpose. The encounter with this righteous second soul may aid a living person achieve perfection. Thus, the benign possession may strengthen the good qualities and heighten the consciousness—the physical, emotional, intellectual, or spiritual development—of a living person. By providing information and guidance regarding present and future events, the second soul also may offer helpful assistance to a living human being.

A benign possession, as a form of temporary reincarnation, may, Jewish mystics taught, also help the soul of a righteous departed one whose purification has almost been attained to avoid the need for reincarnation. By entering the soul of a living person, the disembodied soul can perform one or more good deeds, words, or thoughts, thus receiving the merit requisite to overcome its past transgressions. The beneficent conduct, words, or thoughts of the living person may also assist the soul repair its imperfections.

Generally, after the righteous soul completes its mission, it returns to the spirit realms. Throughout the experience of a benign possession, the Jewish sages indicate that the soul of the living person does not experience the pains of the possessed and maintains its own independence.

Because of the magnitude of sins committed during life, some souls were seen as barred from reincarnation. Although these souls pleaded to enter Purgatory, they were so tainted and defiled that the angels guarding the gates refused permission for entry.

In Jewish folklore and popular belief from the seventeenth century onward, this type of soul—called a dybbuk—did not rest peacefully but was left at the mercy of the angels who forced it to wander in limbo. Ultimately, the dybbuk, a wandering, clinging soul, sought a haven in and invaded the body of a living person it could call its own. The dybbuk—an evil, vengeful possession—and its victim were viewed as coexisting in the victim's body.

Evil spirits came to possess receptive individuals who may have committed one or more hidden sins, thereby opening their weakened souls to the dybbuk. Generally speaking, the dybbuk was seen as an evil influence, taking hold of a living person in a variety of rather terrifying ways, such as causing mental illness. Prior to modern times, Jewish mystics assumed that individuals with emotional problems were possessed by evil spirits.

Through an evil possession by a dybbuk, a demonic soul took over a living person's physical body and mind, shattering or disrupting him or her and causing trouble both for the human being and the evil spirit. To give a respite to both, the dybbuk had to be exorcised.

A Yiddish play, *The Dybbuk: Between Two Worlds*,[25] tells of Khonen, a young, penniless yeshiva student. Khonen learns that his beloved, Leah, the daughter of a wealthy merchant, is engaged, through an arranged marriage, to an affluent man. In an attempt to become wealthy, the student turns to kabbalistic magic. On hearing of Leah's engagement, Khonen dies, uttering the unpronounceable name of God.

Wedding preparations and the celebration proceed for Leah and her bridegroom. As the moment of betrothal approaches, Leah appears in a trance-like state, concerned about souls and spirits of the deceased. On returning from visiting her mother's grave, Leah becomes possessed. Khonen has returned to possess her as an evil spirit—a dybbuk.

Leah is brought for an exorcism. A magisterial rabbi succeeds in performing the exorcism, and the dybbuk departs from Leah's body. However, just before the wedding ceremony, Leah's soul withdraws from her body and joins her deceased lover in eternal wandering.

---

[25]S. Ansky (1974), *The Dybbuk: Between Two Worlds*, trans. S. Morris Engel (Los Angeles: Nash Publishing). The play written by S. Ansky in 1914, who collected Hasidic tales and folklore as an ethnographer in the Ukraine from 1911–1914.

Dybbuks were expelled by Jewish rites of exorcism that comprised a form of soul reparation.[26] A charismatic scholar known as a master of the Divine name (a Baal Shem) performed the exorcism. The rite consisted of reciting various prayers and psalms (most importantly, Psalm 91) and diverse incantations, including different combinations of God's name, and offering the promise of atonement for the dybbuk. The rite also included sounding a shofar (a ram's horn) and displaying seven Torahs (parchment scrolls on which the biblical Five Books of Moses are handwritten), burning black candles, as well as a shroud. The exorcist also often administered sulphurous fumes to the possessed's nose to open the spirit's mouth so it would disclose its name and exit the victim's body. A public ordering of the oppressed spirit to depart together with intense prayer often brought about the hoped for influence of Divine energies on the dybbuk. After the successful expulsion of the dybbuk, most victims were revitalized and exhibited a marked improvement in their physical or mental condition.

Through the experience of possession and exorcism, the wandering soul was viewed as achieving a greater or lesser degree of purification, depending on the circumstances which had compelled the soul back to earth to engage in the evil possession. After its purification, the soul could return to its wandering, perhaps journeying through Purgatory, Paradise, the Divine Treasury, and finally experiencing rebirth in a human body.

THE ULTIMATE DESTINATION: UNION WITH GOD

With new opportunities for performing good deeds, expressing kind words, and thinking beneficent thoughts on earth, reincarna-

---

[26]Nigal, *Magic*, pp. 107–133; Winkler, *Soul*, 67–85.

tion enables a soul to fully actualize its potential and attain a higher degree of physical, emotional, intellectual, and spiritual perfection. Successive rebirths enable a soul to evolve and obtain a sense of the more profound dimensions of God. As a soul continually reincarnates, it ultimately achieves complete purification and perfection.

For the mystics, the soul gradually progresses to its final goal: union with God, thereby ending its cycles of birth and death in the earthly world.[27] If we view the Holy One as an independent Being, then perhaps the concept of union with the Divine may best be seen as touching God or as merging an individual's will with the will of God so that the two are essentially the same.

In the soul's long and arduous spiritual journey, time is a relative criterion. Some righteous souls achieve the desired realization of a spiritual life, union with God, much sooner than others.

USING TRADITIONAL JEWISH RITUALS TO FACILITATE THE SOUL'S AFTERLIFE JOURNEY

As discussed in Chapter 8, two Jewish rituals, first, the recitation of the Mourner's Prayer (Kaddish) annually on the anniversary of the death of a parent (or other close relative), and second, the recitation of the prayers offered at four annual memorial (*Yizkor*) services, serve to strengthen the bond between the living and the soul of the departed.

Based on the premise that a window of communication exists between the survivors and the soul of a deceased individual, saying the Mourner's Kaddish prayer and regularly participating in communal memorial prayer services heighten the interconnection between the living and the dead. As previously discussed on page 207 of Chapter 8, a survivor hopes that through his or her prayers, the

---

[27]Raphael, *Afterlife*, p. 326; Gershom, *Beyond the Ashes*, p. 187.

soul, while in the Storehouse of the Souls prior to rebirth, will continue to be a good pleader for the living in the Divine realm which, in turn, will lead to positive earthly repercussions.

SUGGESTIONS FOR SPIRITUAL SEEKERS

Because of the ongoing relationship between the living and the soul to be implanted, at some point, in a fetus (or after birth, in a baby), strive to enhance the linkage between this world and the worlds beyond. Set aside time for reflection and connection (or reconnection) at least annually on the anniversary of the death (or birth) of a parent (or other close relative). Try to communicate with the soul periodically on one or more other special occasions throughout the year. Continue to build on the sense of partnership previously established in the relationship with the soul of a departed.

As discussed in Chapter 8, to remain in contact with a soul, spend time in unstructured individual prayer, silent meditation, or visualization. Through spontaneous, personal prayer, strive to reach out to God. Pour out heartfelt feelings and continue to seek compassion and mercy for the departed spirit on its postmortem journey.

Utilizing the Forgiveness and Lovingkindness Meditation (or Visualization) set out on pages 179–180, send forgiving and loving messages to the soul. Also, using the Remembrance Visualization, set out on pages 211–212 in Chapter 8, remember a beloved and strive to assist its soul in the postdeath realms. These techniques will strengthen the interconnectedness between the living and the soul of a departed loved one, helping prepare the soul for its earthly rebirth.

Even after reincarnation, a linkage remains. If reincarnated, whatever we dedicate on the deceased's behalf will benefit him or her by removing obstacles in his or her new life and furthering his or her emotional, intellectual, and spiritual progress. Loved ones can attain additional merit for a reincarnated soul through their good thoughts, words, and deeds.

Because all of us face the difficulties, hardships, and adversities of life, realize that every situation and experience in our lives contains the seeds for our good and for our spiritual benefit. Life's difficulties are given to us for a reason. Handled "correctly," through the process of trial and error, these experiences make us stronger, more knowledgeable, and more perceptive. No matter how hidden, each of us should strive to find a response to each difficulty and each hardship we encounter that is creative, growth-oriented, and life-affirming. Times of challenge represent an exceptional opportunity to rediscover the lasting truth of our deeper spiritual nature. Thus, we can all discover the message of life within the meaning of death.

CHAPTER TEN

THE MESSAGE OF LIFE WITHIN THE MEANING OF DEATH: INNER PEACE FOR DAILY LIVING

The Jewish tradition's views about death, the postdeath survival of the immortal soul, and rebirth provide comfort, helping to heal your heart and your emotional hurt and to quench your thirsting soul.

The Jewish tradition affirms a belief in life after death. Each individual's timeless immortal soul survives bodily death. Because death represents a transition to another state of consciousness do not fear the end of earthly existence. With the demise of the physical body, a person's soul enters a spiritual world and undergoes a series of transformational experiences designed to purify the soul and facilitate its emotional, intellectual, and spiritual evolution.

As we saw in Chapter 4, an acceptance of death was common among the pious Jews of old. Life and death were viewed as fulfilling God's destiny for each person. The devout embraced God equally in life and death. They saw the interconnectedness between the world of the living and the world of souls.

Those who accepted God's grace into their lives had no fear of death. According to one Hasidic legend, Rabbi Elimelech—one of the leading figures in the Hasidic movement, who developed the idea of making the personality of a zaddik (an accomplished, righteous rabbi) the focal point of a disciple's existence—was extraordinarily cheerful as he approached death. In response to a disciple who asked for an explanation of his unusual mood, he replied:

> "Why should I not rejoice, seeing that I am about to leave this world below, and enter into the higher worlds of eternity? Do you not recall the words of the Psalmist: 'Though I walk through the valley of shadow of death, I will fear no evil, for You are with me' (Psalms 23:4). Thus does the grace of God display itself."[1]

Reflecting on Reb Elimelech's response, hopefully death holds no terror for us. Our fear of annihilation diminishes, if not vanishes. Instead, death marks the start of a new journey in realms free from earthly hindrances.

Our concept of what will happen to us after death impacts on how we lead our lives in the here and now. Our thoughts about death represent a reawakening.

Imagine you're driving home from work tomorrow evening. You see the flash of lights in your car's rearview mirror, you hear the screech of the brakes of the car behind, and the shattering impact of a rearend collision. Darkness descends on you.

Imagine how you would have wished to live your life. What's really important? What would you resolve to change or to do better?

As a spiritual seeker, honestly and directly face the fact of your finiteness in life on this earthly plane. Despite the technological advances of modern medicine, it is absolutely certain that you *will* die; what is unclear is *when* and *how*. Suddenly, in a car accident;

---

[1] *The Hasidic Anthology: Tales and Teachings of the Hasidim*, ed. and trans. Louis I. Newman (Northvale, NJ: Jason Aronson, 1987), p. 70.

tomorrow; or, after a long, slow, painful illness many years in the future.

Recognizing the impermanence of the material world, from our possessions to our physical bodies, opens new possibilities for our lives, here and now. Impermanence affords a new level of responsibility and choice. Realize that we're spiritual beings in a spiritual world. There's more to our existence than our physical bodies and present earthly life.

As you open the essence of your being to life, both now and in the hereafter, let's return to Spiritual Judaism's guideposts for living, as developed in Chapter 2. Let's focus on practical techniques for cultivating love and compassion and enhancing forgiveness.

TECHNIQUES TO CULTIVATE LOVE AND COMPASSION

On a daily basis, it's important to practice choosing unconditional love and compassion. Be love's instrument, minute by minute, each and every day, from the beginning of your day until day's end.

Begin your day with love for everyone. Remember that you and all of humanity are one. Each of us has the same life flow. There is the same Divinity in each of us. Because we are one, we must feel one. Begin the day with love, with thoughts of goodness, kindness, and compassion for everyone.

It's important for each of us to develop love and compassion through actual practice, on a daily basis. Nothing binds heart to heart more closely than an act of kindness, or links soul to soul more firmly than a tender word. Nothing brings more cheer than a sympathetic thought.

During the day, be a helper to all; an enemy to none. Extend love to everyone you come into contact with. Consciously cultivate lovingkindness and bring it into your thoughts, actions, and words.

Overlook the weaknesses in others. Don't dwell on their faults or their negatives.

Don't harbor bitterness or hatred in your heart. Don't erect barriers that keep your heart isolated from others. Don't close your heart in fear, judgment, criticism, or anger. When your heart is closed, you're cut off from the flow of love. If the flow of love is blocked, you'll experience fear and pain.

In your thoughts and in your heart, see only the good that exists in others. A sympathetic interpretation of others' deeds and words will show you their better and finer nature.

Remember that Divine attributes exist in each of us. There's goodness in every heart and nobility in every soul. See only the good and the Divine in others and the good and the Divine will express themselves to you.

Each day strive to perform small acts of gentleness, kindness, and patience, one building upon another. Through your acts seek to bring out the best and the highest in others, to elevate others, and to encourage and inspire others in their efforts. Through your deeds give others dignity and respect.

During the day, don't speak ill of anyone for any reason. As my parents emphasized, "If you don't have anything good to say about someone, keep quiet." Good advice.

Train your tongue to speak kind words. Speak kindly to people and of people. Speak kind words. Words that encourage, that bring out the best in others, that inspire others to higher achievements and better conduct, and that offer expressions of appreciation, not words that hurt or humiliate.

Speaking a kind word kindles hope in the despondent. It lifts up the dejected, creates friendship even in the hearts of enemies, and transforms enmity into love.

A kind word leaves a lasting, positive impression. You'll encourage others, giving them strength. You'll gain their respect and admiration.

Ask yourself whether there are important people in your life whom you haven't told how much you love and value them? Perhaps, you've told them, but not recently or sufficiently? If so, call, write a note, or send an e-mail expressing your appreciation to each of them.

Each day remember, also, that we live to serve others, to benefit humanity. Dedicate part of your existence to helping humanity through selfless service to others.

Each day reach out to those around you by being of service to others. Ask what can you do best for others to make their lives easier, to relieve their suffering, and to help them experience happiness by kindling hope in their hearts and comforting them in their pain.

On a more concrete level, offer your time, your prayers, your compassion, your counsel and advice, your talents, and your money. Volunteer to help individuals or organizations even for a few hours each month, thereby bringing joy to people suffering from the pain of loneliness, homelessness, hunger, or sickness.

In making decisions, reflect on the goal of unconditional love and selfless service to others. Each day, ask: How much love am I giving? How much service am I rendering?

By considering and devoting yourself to others, you not only demonstrate your oneness with all of humanity but also affirm that each person is part of the ongoing process of planetary creation and healing. By recognizing our common humanity, together we can help create a better world. Each of us, in performing beneficent deeds, speaking kind words, and fulfilling our own highest good, brings us nearer to the healing of the world, the tradition of *Tikkun Olam* in Hebrew.

Each night before you go to sleep, think of one or more acts of lovingkindness and selfless service you performed during the day. You may want to keep a journal of your deeds of lovingkindness, compassion, and service, perhaps organized by various categories. You may wish to send a silent blessing to those you love, perhaps to all earthly beings, and even to people you've found difficult to get along with.

Each evening also contemplate your missed opportunities for expressing lovingkindness and selfless service, in words or deeds. Cultivate your awareness of these missed opportunities, the various needs of others, and the possibilities for being of service to others.

Through speaking kind words and performing acts of goodness, the habit of love will become the deepest part of your being, replacing the habit of criticism, fears, and suspicion.

As you fill your heart with love for everyone, implementing your feelings through words and conduct, people will respond with love. Kindness reaches the heart and stimulates love. The more you love, the more you'll be loved in turn. You'll find yourself linked to the hearts of others. As the saying goes, "Everything that goes around comes around." Every outpouring stream of love and compassion brings back joy and happiness.

TECHNIQUES TO FACILITATE FORGIVENESS

As you contemplate how to forgive, to gently reopen your heart to love and let go of the way you're looking at a situation, a relationship, or a human interaction, sincerely ask God to guide and direct your thought, perception, and understanding.

There's no magic formula for forgiveness. Don't try to figure out how to accomplish or express forgiveness in any situation or relationship.

Trust that the Holy One will show you the way. Recognize that you're not fully in charge. Surrender and align yourself with the Divine Will. Recognize that closing your heart to love results in pain; choosing to forgive will release you from this pain. Have faith in another's spiritual identity and essence as a child of God. If you ask God with sincerity, you will receive a new vision of another human being and the way to inner peace.

Many have found the Forgiveness Meditation helpful in forgiving others to whom the heart has been closed or in asking others for their forgiveness. Use this meditation, twice daily, in the morning and evening, for ten to fifteen minutes at each session.

Forgiveness Meditation

Introductory Instructions. Try to create a warm, welcoming atmosphere, an environment of serenity and spaciousness for the journey within. Lower the lights, if possible, in your room. Candles can set a mood that enhances meditation.

Close your eyes, sit quietly, calm and relax your body by sitting, reclining or lying down. Breathe in and out normally, feeling where the breath flows into and out of the body. Adjust the breaths so that the in and out breaths are the same length thereby bringing about both a relaxation of the body and an alertness of the mind.

Feel yourself surrounded by warmth and patience.

Allow any anger you feel toward others dissolve into the warmth and patience.

With each breath, breathe in warmth.

Feel the warmth nourishing you.

Breathe in patience and feel the spaciousness and the opening of your heart that patience creates within.

Allow the warmth and patience to give rise to forgiveness.

The power of forgiveness is great.

Release yourself from any tension or tightness you feel inside, caused by resentment.

Let go of the pride that holds onto resentment.

Allow the pain of old hurts to fade away.

Reflect on someone who has caused you pain, intentionally or unintentionally, and send him/her forgiveness.

Forgive him/her as best you can.

Allow the forgiveness to grow.

Let go of your judgment of another, and replace it with understanding and compassion.

Allow the resentment to fade away.

For another whom you have caused pain and suffering, ask for his/her forgiveness.

Forgive yourself for anyone's pain and suffering you have contributed to.

Concluding Instructions. Come back to the here and now. Take time to ease yourself back. Slowly bring your awareness back into your body. Feel yourself back in the room and open your eyes.

Cause and effect, which has an important role in our existence and in the universe, has a long trajectory regarding forgiveness. Everything you do, think, and speak represents a productive cause, impacting you and those around you. As you forgive others so, in turn, you will be forgiven now and in the world of souls. In every situation, you should remain open to the healing, the inner peace, and the freedom that forgiveness offers.

SOME CONCLUDING THOUGHTS

Always remember to look at life and death as a whole. They're an inseparable part of a continuum. If you really understand death and accept the notion of an afterlife, you'll have a different perspective on life.

Each day, be sensitive to the immediate and long-term consequences, large and small, of our thoughts, words, and deeds. Each human existence on the planet and in the world of the souls is intertwined. Helping or harming others will come back to each of us, now or in the hereafter. If we act and speak positively, we bring to others happiness and to ourselves future happiness. Conversely, if we harm others, we harm ourselves, now and in the hereafter.

Realizing the impermanence of life and the pervasiveness of change, death represents an opportunity for the transformation of the soul and ultimately for rebirth. However much we wish to cling to life and our physical body, we need to accept the reality of death and change our behavior by forgiving and letting go of the past. Let us be inspired to abandon our grasping, our greed, and our desires, and to be free from our temporary material attachments. However, never give up our unconditional love and compassion, our ability to forgive others, and our humility.

Spiritual Judaism offers a message of hope and inspiration now, during the process of dying, at death, and in the afterlife. The Jewish tradition is one of eternal optimism. The Psalmist never lost hope. Sustained by faith in God's goodness and help, the Jewish people have never given up hope. Optimism is difficult for many in the post-Holocaust world; it is especially hard when illness with its accompanying pain and suffering are close at hand, when the future looks ever so bleak.

Faith in God that all will be well, that the Eternal's goodness and mercy will never fail, represents one of the outstanding teachings of Judaism. Optimism, grounded in faith and trust, helps assure us that God did not create each of us only to destroy us. God won't uproot what was planted.

Spiritual optimism is important as we face suffering and evil in life and ultimately, death. Spiritual optimism helps us to overcome our despair and to feel that the cosmos we inhabit is not a chance cluster of material particles and energy that accidentally gave rise to life and mind. Rather, view the universe as basically good; a purposeful and friendly place for the unfolding of consciousness. The cosmos serves as an arena for the evolution of the spirit, a place where our individual and our collective efforts can make a difference. Thus, strive to help God complete the Divine plan of creation.

Recognizing that what is possible can be attained, spiritual optimism challenges us to be life-affirming. Spiritual optimism motivates us to encourage the spark of goodness within each of us by helping each individual realize his or her highest self. Now while we're alive, we should say to ourselves and to others, "Go for the Light."

If you feel yourself acting or speaking in an unloving, unforgiving, or pessimistic manner, ask yourself, "What am I doing or saying?" Tell yourself, "Hold it, I'm doing or saying it again. I must make a choice." It's your choice. This is where your will, your discipline comes in.

Focus on the ethics and virtues of Spiritual Judaism, as developed in Chapter 2. Align yourself with these values as your guiding force. This may be quite difficult initially. You may let yourself give in to your old values and perceptions.

Strive, however, to develop your internal discipline. Say to yourself: "Instead of this, I choose love, forgiveness, and inner peace." If you don't like the experience you're having, the words you're expressing, or the deeds you're doing, you can decide that you want to say or do something else.

Always remember, as you go through life, not to grow weary or become disillusioned. Never give up hope. Judaism teaches us to be joyous. Interpret life in positive terms. Discipline your mind to escape the grasp of misery. Train your heart to shut out discouragement. See life's traumas as challenges, not threats. Try to exert some measure of control when facing problems that are in some way solvable rather than allowing yourself to become helpless or hopeless.

As Rabbi Nachman of Breslov—the great-grandson of the Baal Shem Tov, who roused his followers to unknown heights of attachment to God coupled with joy—reminds us:

Never despair! Never!

It is forbidden to give up hope.[2]

---

[2] *The Empty Chair: Finding Hope and Joy*, adapted by Moshe Mykoff and The Breslov Research Institute (Woodstock, VT: Jewish Lights Publishing, 1994), p. 110.

SELECTED BIBLIOGRAPHY

Aaron, David (1997), *Endless Light: The Ancient Path of the Kabbalah to Love, Spiritual Growth, and Personal Power.* New York: Simon and Schuster.

Berg, Philip S. (1984*)*, *The Wheels of a Soul: Reincarnation: Your Life Today—and Tomorrow.* New York: Research Centre of Kabbalah.

Brener, Anne (1993), *Mourning & Mitzvah: A Guided Journal for Walking the Mourner's Path Through Grief to Healing.* Woodstock, VT: Jewish Lights Publishing.

Buber, Martin (1947), *Tales of the Hasidim: The Early Masters*, trans. Olga Marx. New York: Schocken.

——— (1948) *Tales of the Hasidim: The Later Masters*, trans. Olga Marx. New York: Schocken.

Cooper, David A. (1997*)*, *God Is A Verb: Kabbalah and the Practice of Mystical Judaism.* New York: Riverhead.

Diamant, Anita (1998). *Saying Kaddish: How to Comfort the Dying, Bury the Dea, and Mourn as a Jew.* New York: Schocken.

Doore, Gary, ed. (1990), *What Survived? Contemporary Explorations of Life After Death.* Los Angeles: Jeremy P. Tarcher.

Dossey, Larry, M.D. (1989), *Recovering the Soul: A Scientific and Spiritual Search.* New York: Bantam.

Friedman, Richard Elliott (1987), *Who Wrote the Bible?* Englewood Cliffs, N.J.: Prentice Hall.

Gershom, Yonassan (1992), *Beyond the Ashes: Cases of Reincarnation from the Holocaust.* Virginia Beach, VA: A.R.E. Press.

——— (1996) *From Ashes to Healing: Mystical Encounters with the Holocaust.* Virginia Beach, VA: A.R.E. Press.

Glynn, Patrick (1997), *God: The Evidence: The Reconciliation of Faith and Reason in a Postsecular World.* Rocklin, CA: Forum.

Guggenheim, Bill and Judy (1996), *Hello From Heaven!: A New Field of Research, After-Death Communication, Confirms That Life and Love Are Eternal.* New York: Bantam.

Hertz, Joseph H. (1985), *The Authorised Daily Prayer Book*, rev. ed. New York: Bloch.

Hodgkinson, Liz (1989), *Reincarnation: The Evidence.* London: Piatkus.

Kübler-Ross, Elisabeth (1991), *On Life After Death.* Berkeley, CA: Celestial Arts.

——— (1997) *The Wheel of Life: A Memoir of Living and Dying.* New York: Scribner.

Lamm, Maurice (1969), *The Jewish Way in Death and Mourning.* New York: Jonathan David.

Levine, Stephen (1982), *Who Dies? An Investigation of Conscious Living and Conscious Dying.* Garden City, NY: Anchor.

Lichenstein, Morris (1934), *Judaism: A Presentation of Its Essence and a Suggestion for Its Preservation.* New York: Society for Jewish Science.

Longaker, Christine (1997), *Facing Death and Finding Hope: A Guide to the Emotional and Spiritual Care of the Dying*. New York: Doubleday.

Mintz, Jerome R. (1968), *Legends of the Hasidim: An Introduction to Hasidic Culture and Oral Tradition in the New World*. Chicago: University of Chicago Press.

Mishove, Jeffrey (1993), *The Roots of Consciousness: The Classic Encyclopedia of Consciousness Studies Revised and Expanded*. Tulsa: Oak Council Books.

Moody, Raymond A., Jr. (1976), *Life After Life*. New York: Bantam.

Moody, Raymond A., Jr., with Paul Perry (1988), *The Light Beyond*. New York: Bantam.

——— (1993) *Reunions: Visionary Encounters with Departed Loved Ones*. New York: Villard.

Newman, Louis I., ed. and trans. (1987), *The Hasidic Anthology: Tales and Teachings of the Hasidim*. Northvale, NJ: Jason Aronson.

Nigal, Gedalyah (1994), *Magic, Mysticism, and Hasidism: The Supernatural in Jewish Thought*, trans. Edward Levin. Northvale, N.J.: Jason Aronson.

Paull, Simcha Steven [Simcha Raphael] (1986), *Judaism's Contribution to the Psychology of Death and Dying*. Ph.D. diss., California Institute of Integral Studies.

Rabinowicz, Tzvi (1989), *A Guide to Life: Jewish Laws and Customs of Mourning*. Northvale, NJ: Jason Aronson.

Raphael, Simcha Paull (1994), *Jewish Views of the Afterlife*. Northvale, NJ: Jason Aronson.

Riemer, Jack, ed. (1995), *Jewish Insights on Death and Mourning*. New York: Schocken.

——— (1974) *Jewish Reflections on Death*. New York: Schocken.

Saunders, Cicely and Mary Baines (1989), *Living with Dying: The Management of Terminal Disease*, second ed.. New York: Oxford University Press.

Scholem, Gershom (1991), *On the Mystical Shape of the Godhead: Basic Concepts in the Kabbalah*, ed. Jonathan Chipman, trans. Joachim Neugroschel. New York: Shocken.

Seltzer, Robert M. (1980), *Jewish People, Jewish Thought: The Jewish Experience in History*. New York: Macmillan.

Sonsino, Rifat and Daniel B. Syme (1990), *What Happens After I Die? Jewish Views of Life After Death*. New York: UAHC Press.

Stevenson, Ian (1987), *Children Who Remember Past Lives*. Charlottesville, Va.: University Press of Virginia.

———— (1981) *Twenty Cases Suggestive of Reincarnation*, rev. ed. Charlottesville, Va.: University Press of Virginia.

The Empty Chair: Finding Hope and Joy, adapted by Moshe Mykoff and The Breslov Research Institute. Woodstock, VT: Jewish Lights Publishing, 1994.

Tatelbaum, Judy (1980), *The Courage to Grieve*. New York: Lippincott & Crowell.

Weiss, Brian L. (1988), *Many Lives, Many Masters*. New York: Simon and Schuster.

Wieseltier, Leon (1998), *Kaddish*. New York: Knopf.

Winkler, Gershon (1982), *The Soul of the Matter: A Psychological and Philosophical Study of the Jewish Perspective on the Odyssey of the Human Soul Before, During and After "Life"*. New York: The Judaica Press.

INDEX

ABOUT THE AUTHOR

Lewis D. Solomon, an ordained rabbi, is the Theodore Rinehart Professor of Business Law at The George Washington University Law School, where he has taught corporate and tax law for over twenty years. He holds a B.A. from Cornell University and a J.D. from Yale Law School, and is a member of the Bar of the State of New York. Rabbi Solomon received his ordination from the Rabbinical Studies Department of The New Seminary and has served as a guest rabbi at Jewish houses of worship and has officiated at numerous life cycle events. He is a member of the Rabbinical Fellowship of America, International and is the author (or co-author) of more than thirty books and fifty articles. Rabbi Solomon has taught courses on Jewish Views of the Afterlife and Basic Judaism and lectures on Jewish Spirituality. He resides in Washington, D.C. with his wife Jane Stern Solomon. They have one son, Michael.